Feelings

A course in conversational English for upper-intermediate and more advanced students

Teacher's Book

Adrian Doff and Christopher Jones

Cambridge University Press
Cambridge
London   New York   New Rochelle
Melbourne   Sydney

Published by the Press Syndicate of the University of Cambridge
The Pitt Building, Trumpington Street, Cambridge CB2 1RP
32 East 57th Street, New York, NY 10022, USA
296 Beaconsfield Parade, Middle Park, Melbourne 3206, Australia

© Cambridge University Press 1980

First published 1980

Reprinted 1983

Printed in Great Britain
at the University Press, Cambridge

ISBN 0 521 21846 2 Teacher's Book
ISBN 0 521 21847 0 Student's Book
ISBN 0 521 21845 4 Cassette

Contents

Foreword 4

Introduction 6
Linguistic background 7
Organisation of each unit 12
General methodological notes 12
Further notes: grammar; functions; intonation; examinations 15

Teaching notes 17
Unit 1: Desire/Longing 18
Unit 2: Excitement/Anticipation 33
Unit 3: Worry/Apprehension 42
Unit 4: Admiration 50
Unit 5: Irritation/Impatience 59
Unit 6: Delight/Relief 67
Unit 7: Indignation/Annoyance 76
Unit 8: Surprise 86
Unit 9: Disappointment/Regret 94
Unit 10: Interest/Curiosity 102
Unit 11: Uncertainty 111
Unit 12: Sympathy and Lack of sympathy 120

Appendices
A The scope of each unit 129
B Adjectives and verbs used to describe feelings 133
C The cassette 135

Foreword

If someone says 'I wish you'd stop biting your fingernails all the time', is he nervous, irritated, angry or furious?

If you had been eating fish and chips every night for the past two weeks, would you be feeling fed up, dissatisfied, disappointed or disillusioned?

If you saw a beautiful sunset, would you admire it, praise it, compliment it or congratulate it?

You had a row with your neighbour yesterday. Tell a friend exactly what happened.

In what situations might you use these formulae?
a) How dare you! b) That's all I need! c) Have it your own way!

'I've told you twice already — five to four.' What is the person talking about, and how is he feeling?

If you regretted buying a flat would you say 'I wish I . . . it'
a) didn't buy b) haven't bought c) hadn't bought?

What is the difference between 'I'm waiting to see Jack' and 'I can hardly wait to see Jack'?

You came to work late, and your boss didn't notice you come in. Tell someone how relieved you are, and why.

What are the differences between:
a) 'Would you shut that door?' and 'Shut that door, can't you?'
b) 'Why did he go?' and 'Whatever made him go?'

You have ordered a book from a bookshop, and you call in to ask about it. Do you say to the assistant 'Isn't it about time my book arrived?' or 'I was wondering whether my book had arrived yet'? Why?

Tell someone you want a drink in these situations:
a) you're a bit thirsty. b) you're extremely thirsty.

You're in a car crash, and you think it is the other driver's fault. What might you say to him? How might the argument develop?

These questions illustrate some of the ways in which feelings are both described and expressed in everyday conversation. Since the structures used to express feelings vary considerably from one language to another, this is a major area of difficulty for foreign learners of English, even those who have reached an advanced level. This course was developed to teach systematically the language used both to express feelings and to describe feelings. It teaches students:

1 How to talk about feelings and situations involving feelings. This involves
   i) different expressions used to describe feelings, and the differences in meaning between them.
   ii) narrative skills, especially for describing an incident from a particular point of view.

2 How to understand which feelings are being expressed by other people. This involves
   i) typical formulae for expressing feelings.
   ii) relating isolated remarks to an appropriate situation.

3 How to express feelings. This involves
   i) structures and formulae for expressing feelings.
   ii) language used for other functions but which also shows a particular feeling (e.g. accusing, reassuring, thanking, apologising, etc.).
   iii) using language appropriate to a situation, according to strength of feeling, role relationship, topic, etc.
   iv) extended student—student interaction, using a wide variety of language functions in a wide variety of situations.

Introduction

Who the book is for

Feelings is intended for upper-intermediate and more advanced students of English who already have a good grasp of the structures of English, but who need practice in expressing themselves fluently in everyday situations. It can be used towards the end of secondary school, in universities and in language institutes.

The Student's Book

The Student's Book consists of twelve units, each dealing with one broad area of feeling. Units are in two parts: in *part one* of each unit students learn how to talk about feelings and situations involving feelings; in *part two* of each unit they learn how to recognise other people's feelings and express feelings themselves.

The course provides a variety of stimulating material which encourages students to be imaginative and creative. Many of the activities are for use in pairs and small groups, and include role-play, simulation, discussion, problem-solving and game activities.

Recorded material

The course is accompanied by a cassette recording. This contains the introductory dialogues for part one of each unit, and material for recognition exercises in part two of each unit. The symbol ▣ beside an exercise indicates that it is on tape; a list of these exercises is given in appendix C, p. 135.

Length of the course

Each unit provides material for 6–7 classroom hours, making a total of approximately 70–80 hours. The course could be used in the following ways:
a) as a 6–8 week intensive course (10–15 hours per week).
b) as a 12-week semi-intensive course (6–7 hours per week).
c) as a non-intensive course taught parallel to a general English course.

Introduction

d) as supplementary material to a general English course.

Linguistic background

This is in two parts: 1 The language of feelings; 2 Indirect language.

1 The language of feelings

A definition of feelings

Gilbert Ryle, in his book *The Concept of Mind*, divides what people refer to informally as 'feelings' into three general categories:
1 *'Tendencies'* (e.g. 'He's a *cynical* person', 'I'm *interested* in physics') Tendencies are features of character. They are more or less permanent, and although they may affect how a person feels in a particular situation, they are not themselves bound to any situation.
2 *'Moods'* (e.g. 'It made him feel very *cynical*', 'I'm feeling *lazy* this morning') Moods, unlike tendencies, are temporary; they come and go, and may be related to a particular event.
3 *'Agitations'* (e.g. 'How *fascinating*!', 'I was suddenly overcome by *curiosity*') Agitations are also strictly temporary, and closely bound to a particular situation. But unlike moods, they completely dominate a person's mind for as long as they last; they are in many ways similar to sudden physical sensations of heat, pain, etc. Agitations are often talked about in physical terms (e.g. 'He was *burning* with anger'), and accompanied by physical 'symptoms' such as blushing, quivering, clenching fists, frowning, etc.

In terms of language and language teaching, it is only the last of these three categories that is of any importance. 'Tendencies' are not themselves expressed in language at all, although they may certainly affect the kinds of things a person is likely to say. For example, a cynical person might be expected to use certain kinds of language (e.g. to criticise, cast doubt, ridicule) more frequently than people who are not cynical, but it is impossible to identify any particular language as 'the language used by cynical people'. 'Moods' will affect what a person says more strongly than 'tendencies', but again they are not directly expressed in language except by simple performative expressions. It is impossible, for instance, to pinpoint any language that specifically expresses 'laziness', other than 'I feel lazy' or 'I'm in

Introduction

a lazy mood'. 'Agitations', however, are quite a different matter. They are regularly and productively expressed in language, and it is possible to identify particular language that is used to express, for example, 'curiosity' or 'worry'.

The syllabus of this book, then, is based only on this last category of 'feelings'.

Organisation of the book

The division of the book into units was preceded by a more general 'mapping' of feelings into the following broad areas:
1 positive and negative feelings about the future (e.g. excitement, apprehension, desire).
2 positive and negative reactions to the present and past (e.g. indignation, delight, irritation).
3 conflict between expectation and reality (e.g. surprise, relief, disappointment).
4 sharing or not sharing other people's feelings (e.g. sympathy, indifference).

With this general framework in mind, we isolated twelve 'types' of feeling, which form the basis of the twelve units. In separating one feeling from another, we tried to avoid relying on names of feelings, since these are often too vague (e.g. 'upset') or too particular (e.g. 'intrigued') to be useful. Instead we tried to 'diagnose' the kind of sensation involved, i.e. what it 'feels like' to have a particular feeling. Thus we included in the unit on 'Delight/Relief' any feeling that involved smiling, lightening of the heart, jumping up and down, etc., and in 'Admiration', any feeling that involved looking wide-eyed, nodding one's head, saying 'Mm!', etc. The *names* which were later given to each unit are intended merely to convey an idea of the range of feelings covered, not as a precise definition.

However, types of feeling are not always clearly distinct from one another; they can, and often do, overlap. We tried to cover complete ranges of related feelings, as well as those that lay between two areas, by exploring the boundaries between each area. Feelings that were on the borderline between two adjacent areas were included in one or both of the areas concerned, (e.g. *annoyance*, which is featured in 'Irritation/Impatience' and 'Indignation/Annoyance'). The points where there is an overlap between units are indicated by the cross-references in the syllabus (appendix A, 'The scope of each unit', p. 129).

Since the book is concerned with the *expression* of feelings, we paid attention only to the feelings expressed, rather than to

Introduction

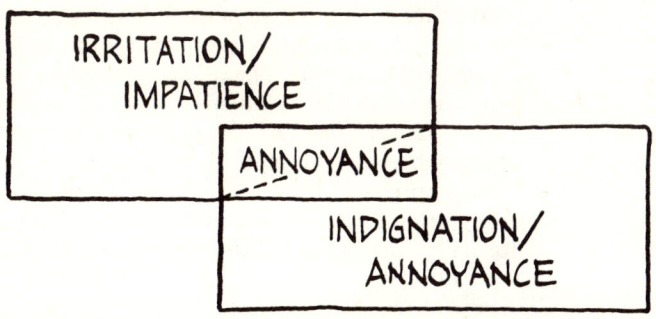

what the speaker may be really feeling 'deep down'. So, for example, *jealousy* has been excluded altogether as a separate feeling, since it is invariably expressed through some other feeling (e.g. *anger* or *suspicion*). Nor have we included situations where the speaker hides his real feeling by expressing another (e.g. assumed excitement to cover nervousness; sarcastic admiration, etc.). In both cases, we have assumed that the strategies involved are not language-specific, and that it is therefore enough to teach the language of the 'surface' feeling.

Feelings with which no productive language is associated have either been omitted altogether, or included only in the indirect language section (part one) of a unit (e.g. terror, boredom).

Selection of exponents

The range of different expressions that can be used to express a feeling is, if not unlimited, at least extremely wide, and this book does not attempt to cover all the possible exponents of any given feeling. It does, however, attempt to cover a wide range of typical situations and of expressions appropriate to them.

In order to define the range of exponents to be included in each unit, we first considered the logically possible combinations of the following parameters:
1 time reference (past, present and future)
2 direction of feeling (towards oneself, interlocutor, other people, things, events, states)
3 extent of feeling (shared by, independent of, or countered by interlocutor(s))
4 'cause' of feeling (speech, activity, state, or lack of any of these)
5 strength of feeling
6 role relationship

Introduction

We then selected exponents according to two criteria — the productivity of language associated with them, and the predicted needs of the student. The practice exercises are limited to situations for which the student is likely to need English, or to other (often 'fantasy') situations which require similar language. Situations where the student might need to recognise the feeling being expressed but not to express it himself are included in the recognition exercises only. Where role relationship and level of formality significantly affect the choice of utterance, exercises are included which emphasise the relevant distinctions.

2   Indirect language

In English, as in other languages, we use two different 'modes' of language:
1 a direct mode, to communicate our thoughts, feelings, etc., in a situation (direct language).
2 an indirect mode, to talk *about* a situation in which communication took place (indirect language).

All teaching of 'indirect speech' is concerned with the ability to use these two modes of language and to 'translate' from one to the other. However, because of the problems of word order and tense usage involved in indirect speech in English, most teaching materials concentrate on the *structure* of indirect speech. This is, of course, extremely important — tense usage is, after all, one of the main problem areas for foreign learners of English. However, simply teaching the structure of indirect speech is not in itself enough to enable the student to use indirect language successfully as a means of communication. The discussion that follows looks at what else is involved in using indirect language, and what the student needs to be taught.

As a starting point, it is important to establish exactly what the purpose of indirect speech is. We use indirect speech to represent to a third person what someone said (or what we said ourselves). It may be used in talking about a meeting with a friend, quoting someone else's opinion, spreading scandal, writing a report on an international conference. But whatever the context, the purpose is always the same — to reconstruct a situation in which communication took place, for the benefit of someone who was not there himself. In doing this, we want to give the third person as accurate a picture as possible of what the conversation was like, without actually acting out the situation for him.

To see how this is achieved, we need to look more closely at

Introduction

the relationship between a direct-speech situation and its representation in indirect language. Anything we say (in a direct-speech situation) is always more than just a grammatically correct sentence. It will also be *appropriate to the situation*: precisely what we choose to say will depend on a whole range of factors, including our relationship to the other speaker, our attitude to him and to the situation, the strength of our feelings, etc. In direct speech, these underlying features remain *implicit* — they are clear from what we say and the way we say it. Imagine, as an example, that a young man is proposing to his girlfriend: he goes down on his knees, wrings his hands in the air, and says '*Please* marry me!' Now the girl will understand from the structure and intonation he uses, as well as from his gestures, the expression on his face, etc., much more than just that he wants to marry her. She can also tell that he is making a request (not a suggestion or a command), that he is desperate, that he considers himself inferior to her. He might go on to say explicitly 'I'm desperate!', but he does not really need to.

When we are talking *about* what somebody said (using indirect language), these clues to the original speaker's feelings and attitudes, and to the situation itself, are no longer available. We are referring to a situation, but neither we nor the listener are in that situation. So a large part of what is *implicit* in direct language has to be made *explicit* in indirect language — otherwise the listener will not get an accurate picture of the original conversation. Thus, if the girl in the example above was telling someone else about her boyfriend's proposal, she would want to convey not only the fact that he had proposed to her, but also the role relationship (inferior–superior) and his feelings (desperation). Clearly it would be inadequate for her to say 'He asked me to marry him' — she would need to say something like 'He begged me to marry him', or better still, 'He went down on his knees and begged me to marry him. He was absolutely desperate.' It is just as important for her to use appropriate language in talking *about* her boyfriend's proposal as it was for her boyfriend to use appropriate language in proposing to her.

Successful communication in indirect language, then, depends to some extent on the use of appropriate verbs which indicate the *kind* of utterance the original speaker made (e.g. suggest, offer, accuse, warn) and the original speaker's *attitude* (e.g. urge, insist, threaten). Often, however, a direct-speech situation (or part of one) is not represented by 'indirect speech' at all, but by a description of the feelings of the speaker, or of what happened, as in these examples:

Introduction

Direct	*Indirect*
'Oh no! not again!'	I was terribly upset when I heard I'd failed the exam.
'Phew!'	He sighed with relief.
'How dare you!'	He was absolutely furious.
'Let's go to the pictures.' 'That's a good idea.'	They decided to go to the pictures.

'Indirect speech' is only one element in a much wider range of 'indirect language', used to make explicit the original speaker's thoughts and feelings, the function of his utterance, and relevant elements in the situation itself.

This ability to 'translate' from a direct to an indirect mode of language is an important part of a native speaker's competence, and is one which foreign learners also need to develop. Here, in summary form, is what the foreign learner would need to be taught, if he is to use indirect language successfully as a means of communication:

1 to use 'indirect speech' structures correctly (tense and word order changes).
2 to use particular verbs of indirect speech appropriately.
3 to use appropriate expressions to describe thoughts and feelings.
4 to use appropriate language to describe actions, events, etc.

Part one of each unit of *Feelings* takes the learner through from a direct-speech situation (the initial dialogue) to writing a report of it, using indirect language. In doing this, it gives students extensive practice in all four of the elements listed above. Least attention is devoted to the first element, as learners at this level are assumed to have mastered the structure of indirect speech already; and most attention is given to the third element, as this also provides the core language for describing feelings.

Organisation of each unit

The table below gives a general picture of the contents of each unit, the activities involved at each stage and the general aims of each part of the unit. Detailed explanations are given in the teaching notes for unit 1, p. 18.

Introduction

PART ONE: TALKING ABOUT THE FEELING

	Activities	General
Section A: Listening and discussion		
Dialogue + questions (facts)	Students listen to a dialogue which illustrates the feeling and discuss the situation behind it.	To teach students:
Multiple-choice questions (language)	Students' attention is focussed on key expressions for talking about the feeling.	1 to talk *about* a feeling.
Section B: Practice		2 to narrate, making effective use of indirect language.
Presentation + exercises	Key language for talking about the feeling is introduced and practised.	
Section C: Reporting	Students write a report, telling the story of what happened in the dialogue.	

PART TWO: EXPRESSING THE FEELING

Section A: Recognition		
Recognition and matching exercises	Students look at/listen to isolated utterances and suggest situations for which they are appropriate.	To give insight into features of style and appropriacy.
Section B: Practice		
Presentation and controlled exercises	Key language for expressing the feeling is introduced and practised.	
Section C: Free expression		To teach students to express a feeling in a given situation.
Free exercises	Students use language they have practised in more extended situations.	

General methodological notes

Feelings is designed to provide as much opportunity as possible for communication in the classroom. For this reason,
1 most of the 'frontal' work (teacher—student interaction, involving the whole class) is in the form of *elicitation*.
2 most of the activities are conducted in *pairs* and *groups*, and consist of student—student interaction.

Introduction

1 Elicitation

The principle of elicitation is that, instead of the teacher giving the class information, with the student as passive listener, the teacher gets the *students* to give as much information as possible themselves. The teacher's role changes from that of instructor to that of guide, prompter and discussion leader.

The use of elicitation enables the teacher
1 to involve the class much more in the activity concerned.
2 to see exactly what students know and do not know, and to adjust his/her teaching accordingly.

In this course, elicitation is used especially for
1 helping students to understand the initial dialogue.
2 checking on students' understanding of structures in the introductory stages of exercises.
3 getting a range of ideas from students as a preparation for role-play.

2 Pairwork and groupwork

In pairwork and groupwork activities, the teacher introduces the exercise to the whole class, and the class is then divided into pairs or small groups (of four or five students). All the pairs or groups conduct the activity at the same time and independently of each other. There may or may not be a round-up stage involving the whole class. During the activity, the teacher goes from pair to pair (or group to group), listening, helping and correcting, as necessary.

The use of pairwork and groupwork is intended
1 to maximise the amount of language used by the students in class.
2 to enable interaction to take place in as 'natural' a situation as possible — i.e. 'privately', and not in front of the whole class.
3 to encourage real communication between students in discussion and problem-solving activities.

In this course, pairwork is used especially for simulation and role-play activities involving two participants.

Groupwork is used especially for
1 simulation and role-play activities involving more than two participants.
2 discussion and problem-solving activities. This is particularly useful where a question has a range of possible answers,

Introduction

which may be reflected in the different answers arrived at by different groups.
3 creative writing activities. A group of students working together will usually produce a more imaginative, and more grammatically correct, piece of writing than an individual student.

Detailed methodological notes are given in the teaching notes for each exercise.

Further notes: grammar; functions; intonation; examinations

Grammar

It is assumed that students who use this course have already mastered the basic structures of English. Because of this grammatical items are *practised* but not *formally presented* in the Student's Book. Difficult grammar points that arise in the exercises are, however, explained in detail in the teaching notes, so that teachers may easily present any items that students are not familiar with.

The following structures are widely used in describing and expressing feelings, and are given extensive practice throughout the course:
sequence of tenses
indirect speech
indirect questions
tag questions
short forms
modals
the unreal past
all types of conditionals
verbs + infinitives and gerunds

Functions

Besides the main functions covered in the course (those concerned with expressing feelings), an extremely wide variety of other interactional functions is practised in part two of each unit. These are of three kinds:
1 functions which are naturally associated with particular feelings:
  e.g. blaming (indignation)

Introduction

    asking for information (curiosity)
    speculating about the past (relief; regret)
2 functions which occur incidentally in role-play situations:
    e.g. agreeing and disagreeing
        persuading and refusing
        making excuses and justifying actions
3 'classroom' functions, which occur in problem-solving and discussion activities:
    e.g. making deductions
        explaining
        giving reasons
        giving opinions

The major language functions involved in each exercise are listed in the teaching notes for each unit (part two, sections B and C).

Intonation

The course does not include any formal teaching of intonation. It is assumed that the teacher can provide an adequate model, and can deal with any serious intonation problems as they arise. Certain recognition exercises draw students' attention to intonation differences where these are particularly important. Most of the recognition exercises are also recorded on the accompanying cassette, and can be used for intonation practice if this is thought necessary.

Examinations

Although *Feelings* is not an examination preparation course, it is useful for students intending to take either the Cambridge First Certificate or Proficiency examinations, in the following areas:

1 *Oral proficiency.* Part two of each unit gives extensive practice both in discussion and in using appropriate language in particular situations.
2 *Informal composition.* Part one of each unit develops narrative skills, particularly the ability to organise events into a coherent story.
3 *Vocabulary development.* Both part one and part two teach systematically vocabulary associated with feelings, and the exercises also include a wide range of more general vocabulary.

Teaching notes

The teaching notes for units 1 and 2 contain detailed procedural notes. Procedural notes for subsequent units refer back to particular exercises in units 1 and 2, except where an exercise type appears for the first time.

The tape will always be required for dealing with the dialogue in part one, section A. For the recognition exercises in part two, section A, the tape may be used as a comprehension aid, or to round up the exercise, or for intonation practice.

Time guide
Part one: 2 lessons (ideally consecutive).
Part two: 4—5 lessons.

Unit 1 Desire/Longing

Part one: Talking about the feeling

Part one of each unit deals with *indirect language*, that is, language used to talk *about* a situation. It begins with a short dialogue which illustrates the feeling dealt with in the unit, and ends with students writing a 'report' of the dialogue, telling the story of what happened. The exercises between the dialogue and the report-writing stage teach language students will need to move from the *direct language* of the dialogue (in which much is left implicit) to the *indirect language* of the report (in which everything must be made explicit). These exercises deal with vocabulary and narrative technique, but especially with ways of describing feelings.

Each part one is divided into three sections:
Section A: Listening and discussion
A1 The dialogue: The dialogue forms the basis for the whole of part one. Most of the exercises which follow refer back to it. It should be emphasised that the dialogue is a piece of listening comprehension, and is intended as a basis for discussion and report-writing. It is *not* intended as material for choral or pair-work repetition.
A2 Facts: These questions are intended as a guide to the teacher as to the points which should be dealt with in the class discussion of the dialogue. This discussion has two purposes:
1 to lead to a full understanding of the dialogue.
2 to elicit particular language for talking about the dialogue. In answering the 'Facts' questions, students are using language which they will need when they write their report later: it is therefore important that they use *appropriate language* to answer them.
A3 Language: These are multiple-choice questions relating to the dialogue, and are mainly concerned with the *feelings of the speakers*. They have two main purposes:
1 to focus attention on useful language for talking about the feelings of the people in the dialogue.
2 to find out which of the expressions students have difficulty

Unit 1 Part one

with. Many of the points arising here are dealt with in the exercises in section B.
Section B: Practice
The exercises in this section have two main purposes:
1 to present a range of words and expressions used to describe the feeling dealt with in the unit, and the differences in meaning between them, and to give students an opportunity of practising them. The range of expressions presented will normally be greater than the range of feelings shown in the dialogue.
2 to present students with specific structures and narrative techniques which will be useful for telling the story of the dialogue.
Section C: Reporting
In this section, students are given final preparation for their report writing, in the form of miscellaneous expressions (many of which are idiomatic), and they then write their reports. They may draw on any of the language introduced in the unit so far: their answers to the 'Facts' and 'Language' questions in section A, the exercises in section B, and the list of expressions in section C. When students write their reports, they will be talking about what people did, felt, thought and said *in the past*. They will therefore need to be familiar with the basic rules of the sequence of tenses, including indirect speech.

SECTION A: LISTENING AND DISCUSSION

A1 Listening and **A2 Facts**
Students listen to the dialogue and discuss what it is about.

Make sure students have their books closed. Play the tape of the dialogue once, and elicit any information the students can give about it, by asking around the class. It is not necessary to go through the 'Facts' questions in order. They are only intended as a guide as to the kind and scope of information to be elicited. As the elicitation continues, the dialogue (or parts of it) may be played again several times, as necessary. The elicitation should not consist solely of seven questions and answers. Sometimes more than one answer is possible, and students should give reasons for their answers, so that a class discussion develops. For example:

Teacher: Can anybody tell me anything about the situation?

Unit 1 Part one

Student A: Yes. They're at a party.
Teacher: Uh huh. Why do you say that?
Student A: Well, there's music . . .
Student B: And there are lots of other people there.
Teacher: Good. How do you know there are other people there?
Student B: Because she says 'Everybody else is'.
Teacher: Fine. Could they be anywhere else?
Student C: Yes. At a discotheque . . .

Students will often give wrong answers. As much as possible, they should be guided towards giving the correct answer themselves. For example:

Teacher: . . . O.K. Now, who do you think they are?
Student D: Husband and wife.
Student E: No, they're not.
Teacher: Why not?
Student E: Well, they don't talk like a husband and wife. She wouldn't explain to him how to dance.
Teacher: So who are they?
Student E: Boyfriend and girlfriend.
Teacher: Have they been going out with each other very long?
Student F: No. It's the first time.
Teacher: Why do you say it's the first time?
Student F: Because she won't go out with him again. She's bored. She wants to dance.
Teacher: Good. How do you know she wants to dance? . . .

When as many of the facts as possible have been established from listening and discussion only, students open their books and follow the dialogue as it is played once more. The 'Facts' questions are then answered very briefly as a summary of the preceding discussion.

Answers
1 Boyfriend and girlfriend. Boy and girl on a date.
2 At a party, discotheque or dance.
3 They're sitting near the dancefloor, watching people dance.
4 She wants to dance.
5 A friend or ex-boyfriend of Janie's, who dances very well.
6 ' . . . really knows how to dance', ' . . . is really fun to go out with', etc.
7 She goes and dances with Roger.

Unit 1 Part one

A3 Language
Students answer multiple-choice questions which are mainly concerned with describing feelings.

These multiple-choice questions concentrate more on the feelings shown in the dialogue. Note that *more than one answer may be correct*, but that there is often a difference in meaning between right answers. For example, in number 1, *a) enjoys dancing* and *c) loves dancing* are both correct, though there is clearly a difference in strength between them.
Wrong answers may be wrong for either of two reasons:
a) they are grammatically incorrect (e.g. 1 b).
b) they are grammatically correct but inappropriate to the situation in the dialogue (e.g. 6 b).
Students are expected to get many of the answers wrong. This is natural, since the language tested has not yet been presented. The purpose these questions serve is to show both students and the teacher exactly what they know and do not know, and this will influence the treatment given to the exercises in section B, which present and practise the key expressions for describing the feeling.

Procedure: Students choose their answers either individually or in pairs. The answers are then gone through and discussed briefly. Where language points which arise are not dealt with in section B following, clear up any difficulties during this discussion. Otherwise, leave discussion to section B.

Answers
1 a,c,d 'Enjoy' is followed by a gerund, 'love' by either gerund or infinitive.
2 b,c
3 a,c,e b = she wouldn't refuse to dance if someone asked her.
         d is archaic in this context.
         f is possible, but extremely strong.
4 b   a = she is successful.
         c and d: 'convince' = 'make someone believe', as in 'He convinced me that he was telling the truth.'
5 a,b,c b is less formal than a and c.
         d and e = he doesn't like dancing *in general*. We can't tell from the dialogue whether this is true.
6 a,c   'won't' here = 'refuses to'.
         b = he thinks about it first and *then* refuses.

Unit 1 Part one

SECTION B: PRACTICE
In this section, key expressions for talking about the feeling are presented and practised.

B1   Strength of feeling

Go through the examples with the students. Point out that the thing the three men want is the same, but their *feelings towards it* differ. Check that students see the difference between the exponents by asking for other examples, or by asking what they themselves are keen/eager/anxious/desperate to do. They then divide up into groups or pairs and decide on the feelings of the people in the exercise, using complete sentences. Go through the answers together.

Answers
1 desperate   4 eager/keen
2 anxious   5 desperate
3 eager/keen   6 anxious

Remind students that their ultimate aim is to be able to report the Janie and Peter incident, by asking them how Janie or Peter might use this language if they were telling someone what happened at the party.

Suggested answers
Both: 'I/She was keen/eager to dance.'

B2   Story line

Most units have a 'Story line' exercise, which provides the students with useful expressions and (especially for weaker students) a framework for part of the story they are going to tell.

The importance of this first 'Story line' exercise is that it shows how the same incident can be reported from *two different points of view*, and that the two story-tellers are likely to choose different language to emphasise their own side of the story.

Procedure: After studying the examples, students form groups and use the same framework to tell the stories indicated by the prompts. Different groups may be assigned different stories. Students must use the expressions in italics in their answers, but are otherwise free to embellish as they wish. (Weaker students will tend to stick closely to the examples, but more imaginative students should be encouraged to be original.) Where a choice of exponents is given, obviously only one is used per

Unit 1 Part one

story, but overall, students sho[uld use]
the expressions in italics. Group[s who finish]
quickly may invent a similar sto[ry using the]
same framework. When all groups [have finished, they tell]
their stories to the class.

As in the previous exercise, the la[nguage prac-]
tised is related to the dialogue:

Janie: 'I was longing to dance, but Pe[ter didn't like]
 the idea. All he wanted to do w[as...]
Peter: 'Janie suddenly decided she wan[ted... I didn't]
 feel like dancing. I was quite cont[ent...]

SECTION C: REPORTING

Students are now almost ready to tell the Janie and Peter story. They have
1 told the story themselves (in the present) in their answers to the 'Facts' questions and the class discussion of the dialogue.
2 practised specific language relevant to the feeling and the dialogue.

C1 *The list.* The list contains *miscellaneous expressions* not met with so far in the unit, which are useful in telling the story of the dialogue. They are not major exponents of the feeling itself and are therefore not given intensive practice. They are intended to help the students *enrich* their story by using natural and idiomatic expressions which are particularly relevant to the dialogue. Some of the expressions would be used by both Janie and Peter in their stories, some not (e.g. Janie would say 'He started making *excuses* . . . ' whereas Peter would be much more likely to say 'I tried to *explain* . . . ').

Procedure: Students suggest ways that either Janie or Peter might use the expressions. Where no one in the class is familiar with an expression, explain it and give an appropriate example.

Suggested answers
1 Peter: 'Janie's crazy about dancing.'   (= she loves it)
2 Peter: 'I didn't fancy dancing.'   (= I didn't feel like it)
 'I think she fancies Roger.'   (= she finds him attractive)
3 Janie: 'I did my best to persuade   (= I tried as hard as I
 him to dance.'   could)

Unit 1 Part one

4 Peter: 'I tried to talk her out of it.' (= to persuade her not to)
5 Janie: 'Peter was obviously embarrassed/got terribly embarrassed,etc.'
  Peter: 'I felt terribly embarrassed.'
6 Peter: 'I think she's just trying to make me jealous.'
  'I'm not jealous or anything, but . . . '
  Janie: 'I think he's jealous of Roger.'
7 Janie: 'He started making excuses.'
  'He made a lot of feeble excuses.'

C2 *Reporting.* Students now write an account of what happened in the dialogue. In their story, they adopt the role of *either* Janie *or* Peter, and the account should be biased towards the storyteller and told from his/her point of view (as in 'Story line', above). This can be done in either of two ways:
a) students write the story individually, as homework.
b) students write the story in class, in groups.
Approximately half the students/groups should adopt one role, the other half the other role. Some of the resulting stories can be read aloud to the class. This is particularly important in this first unit, where students should realise how two narratives of the same incident can differ widely according to attitude.

Point out to the students that they are free to use any of the language they have learnt in the unit, but do not *insist* on them using any particular language in their reports. This should be a completely free exercise. The two reports of the dialogue given below give a rough idea of the kind of report possible. They are not intended as 'models' for students to aim at.

a) Janie: ' . . . And then they all started doing the Hubbly-Bubbly — you remember how I used to dance it with Roger last summer. Well, of course, I was dying to do it again, but Peter didn't seem at all keen on the idea. All he wanted to do was tell me about his university course. I did my best to persuade him to dance, but he just sat there looking embarrassed, and made a lot of silly excuses. Well. I didn't want to sit and talk about poetry with him while everyone else was doing the Hubbly-Bubbly. So when I saw Roger standing at the bar I went and danced with him instead. Of course, as soon as I left the table, Peter jumped up and started calling me back — he's not only a bore, he's jealous too!'

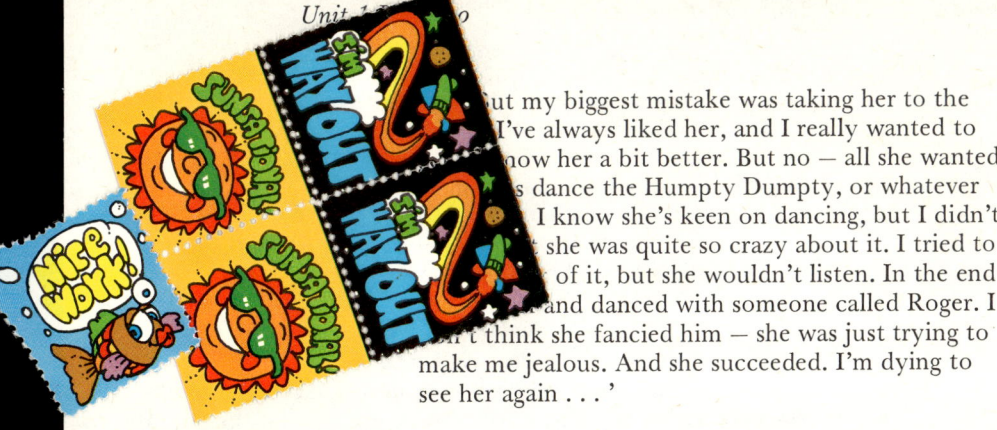

'...ut my biggest mistake was taking her to the ... I've always liked her, and I really wanted to ...ow her a bit better. But no — all she wanted ...s dance the Humpty Dumpty, or whatever ... I know she's keen on dancing, but I didn't ... she was quite so crazy about it. I tried to ... of it, but she wouldn't listen. In the end ... and danced with someone called Roger. I ...t think she fancied him — she was just trying to make me jealous. And she succeeded. I'm dying to see her again . . . '

Part two: Expressing the feeling

SECTION A: RECOGNITION

Exercises in this section have three main purposes:
1 to make students aware of language *in context*, especially features of style and appropriacy (e.g. topic, strength of feeling, formality, relationship between speakers). This is done by students being shown language out of context, and providing the context themselves.
2 to give an opportunity for group discussion in English. This is done by the *problem-solving* nature of the exercises — agreement can only be reached by discussing possible answers (in English!)
3 to familiarise students with useful *formulae* used to express the feeling dealt with in the unit. Many of these students may not need to use themselves, but certainly need to recognise.

Before you begin, explain this to the class, so that they know what they are supposed to be doing. Emphasise that they should *talk* about their answers in English, not merely think about them in their own language.

 A1 Who wants what?

Part two of each unit begins with an exercise like this.

Procedure
Stage 1 Go through the example with the class. Discuss why

25

Unit 1 Part two

                the speaker *must* be talking about a drink ('a drop'), and why it *must* be a reply to what someone else has said ('myself').

Stage 2 Do number 2 together with the class. Encourage them to say as much as possible about the situation, e.g. the two people are disappointed because it's cloudy, they might be on holiday, out for a walk or drive, they wish the weather would improve, the speaker is agreeing with the other person ('Mm'), who might have said 'It's a bit dull today, isn't it?', 'What a pity it's so cloudy today', 'I wish the sun would come out', etc.

Stage 3 Divide the class into small groups, and let them do the rest of the exercise in the same way. Move from group to group helping and checking.

Stage 4 When the first few groups have finished, go through the answers with the whole class. This may be done quite quickly, or may lead to further discussion, depending on your class.

Stage 5 All the remarks are recorded and may be played during the round-up stage at the end.

Answers to numbers 3–8

3 Someone who doesn't like the area, district, etc., he lives in, but has to stay there because of the children's school (or friends). Reply to e.g. 'What's it like living here?'

4 Someone who's very hungry, accepting an offer of some food. Reply to e.g. 'Would you like a sandwich?'

5 Someone who disapproves of workers who go on strike, and wants them to suffer for it. Reply to e.g. 'It looks as if the firm'll go bankrupt if they don't go back to work soon.'

6 Someone who wishes he could give up a bad habit, e.g. smoking, or start a good habit, e.g. going for long walks. Reply to e.g. 'You really ought to give it up.'

7 Someone who is suddenly very interested in a job that he is being offered. Reply to e.g. 'Of course, you wouldn't have any rent to pay. It would be 10,000 a year with a house thrown in.'

8 Someone at a celebration who wants e.g. the guest of honour to make a speech. Might be shouted after the guest has received a prize, present, etc., and has said thank you.

Note: Good classes will usually find plenty to say, and can be left to do exercises like this in groups. You may need to help weaker classes, by, for example, giving them some vocabulary (kids, will power, thrown in) before you begin.

Unit 1 Part two

A2 Best wishes

This is a *matching exercise*. A list of remarks and a list of contexts are given, and students have to match them together. There are exercises like this in most units.

This exercise presents typical formulae for expressing good wishes in letters. Students are asked to distinguish two variables:
1 differences in topic.
2 differences in formality.

Procedure
Stage 1 Introduce the exercise, explaining what it is about and what the class has to do.
Stage 2 Divide the class into small groups or pairs. Let them work fairly quickly through the extracts, finding the pairs (a), (b), (c) and (d), and then deciding which are formal and which are informal. Move from group to group, helping and checking.
Stage 3 Go through the answers with the class. If they have done the exercise fairly quickly, more time can be spent now discussing *how* and *why* the extracts are different. Point out especially:
Full forms: I wish; I hope; may I wish — *formal*
Reduced forms: hoping; wishing; keeping; hope — *informal*

Note: This is a good opportunity to deal with different 'signing off' formulae (e.g. All the best; Yours faithfully; Lots of love).

Answers
1 a) 3,4   b) 1,6   c) 5,7   d) 2,8
2 Yours sincerely, Gerald Fox: 1,2,4,7
  Love, Gerry: 3,5,6,8

SECTION B: PRACTICE

Exercises in this section have two main purposes:
1 to present key expressions used to express the feeling dealt with in the unit.
2 to give intensive practice of these expressions in a variety of different situations, usually (but not always) at the level of single sentences.
   The teaching notes for this section in each unit include:
1 a list of *basic structures*, with references to individual exer-

Unit 1 Part two

cises. This list contains structures which are needed in the exercises, but which are assumed to be known already. If your students do not have a mastery of these structures, they should be practised before you do the exercises.

2 a note on the *language function* of each exercise. This tells you what the language of the exercise is used for, and should be pointed out to the class.

3 notes on *structural difficulties* in individual exercises. These indicate important grammar points that students may not be familiar with, and which are crucial to the exercise. You should always present these, and if necessary do some basic practice on them before proceeding with the exercise.

> *Basic structures*
> *would/could* (B1)
> gerunds + infinitives (B2)
> tag questions (B1)

B1 Wishful thinking

Language function: Wishing for changes.

Structural difficulties: Use of *I wish* and *If only* + *would/could*.
1 *Would* is used about other people/things, *could* about yourself.
2 *I wish* and *If only* mean the same — *If only* tends to be a little stronger. Notice that *If only* can be followed by a single clause to make a complete sentence, e.g. 'If only someone would visit me!' (we don't *have* to continue ' . . . I'd feel happier').
3 *I wish/If only* + *would/could* is used for talking about things you *want to happen* or *want to do*. (cf. *I wish/If only* + past tense, which is used for talking about things you don't like in your *present situation*, and is practised in exercise B3.)

Procedure

Stage 1 After presenting the structures, go through the three pictures (which make a continuous story). Ask students to suggest other things the characters might say: e.g. 'I wish I could get out of here.'
'I wish he'd kiss me.'

Stage 2 Look at the picture of the pavement artist. Ask students

Unit 1 Part two

to suggest things he might be thinking, as represented by the pictures.
Suggested answers
'If only someone would give me a £5 note.'
'I wish that policeman would go away.'
'I wish someone would buy one of my pictures.'
'I wish that policeman would stop staring at me.'
'I wish I could become a famous artist.'
'If only someone would offer to exhibit some of my paintings.'
'If only the sun would come out.'
'I wish it would stop raining.'

Stage 3   The pairwork can be done in two ways: *either* insist on B replying with a tag question, *or* leave B's reply completely open. In either case, go through the examples first, and ask students to suggest other possible replies: e.g. 'Yes, it hasn't rained for a long time, has it?'
   'Yes, a bit of rain would make all the difference, wouldn't it?'
or 'Don't say that – this is the only good weather we've had for months.'

Stage 4   Divide the class into pairs. They improvise two-line conversations for each situation, changing roles each time.

Stage 5   Quickly go through their answers if you think it necessary.

B2   Mild and strong

Language function: Expressing desire for things, mildly and strongly

Structural difficulties: Use of gerund or infinitive after the expressions in the exercise
1 + *noun or gerund*   2 + *infinitive*
   I wouldn't mind . . .   It'd be nice to . . .
   I feel like . . .   I've just got to . . .
   I rather fancy . . .
3 *'mixed' expressions*
   I'm dying *for* + noun/I'm dying *to* + infinitive
   I'd give anything *for* + noun/I'd give anything to + infinitive
   (cf. also *wait for/to, pay for/to, hope for/to, ready for/to*, etc.)

Procedure
Stage 1 Explain the main point of the exercise, which is the different ways you express desire according to (a) how strongly you feel and (b) the kind of person you are. Individually or in pairs, students separate the milder and stronger expressions.
Answers
Humphrey: I wouldn't mind; It'd be nice to; I could do with; I feel like; I rather fancy.
Godfrey: I'm dying for; I've just got to; I'd give anything for.
Stage 2 This part of the exercise brings out the differences in *structural difficulties*, above. Build up three lists on the board, to make them clear.
Stage 3 Divide the class into pairs. Students look at the picture, and improvise as many two-line conversations as they can, agreeing with each other as in the example, and using all the expressions from the list. If you like, give students roles as Humphrey and Godfrey, which they change half way through.

B3 A vicious circle

Language functions: Expressing dissatisfaction with your own situation and envying others; imagining yourself differently.

Structural difficulties: Use of *I wish/If only* + past tense.
This is used for talking about things you don't like in your *present* situation, or imagining yourself differently. It often overlaps with *I wish/If only* + *would/could*. To make the difference clear, it may be worth returning briefly to exercise B1 and giving some contrastive examples:

e.g. 'I wish it *would stop* raining.'   (what you want to
'I wish the sun *would come* out.'   happen)

'I wish it *wasn't* raining.'   (how you'd like things
'I wish the sun *was* out.'   to *be now*)

Procedure
Stage 1 Go through question 1 with the class. Get students to give you as much information as possible, to make the situation clear.
Stage 2 Ask students to suggest things each person might be saying, using expressions from the list (and also from exercise B1 if appropriate):

Unit 1 Part two

    e.g. The peasant: 'I wish I was a servant in the castle.'
            'Wouldn't it be nice to serve wine to the King?'
    Do this fairly quickly, eliciting only one or two sentences for each character, so as to leave scope for the next stage of the exercise.

Stage 3 Divide the class into five groups. Each group takes on the identity of one of the five characters. Each group writes or prepares orally a few *connected* sentences of 'monologue' for their character, using expressions in the box where appropriate.
    A suitable answer for the tramp might be:
    'Oh dear, how I wish I wasn't a tramp! I'd give anything to be that peasant in the field over there. It must be wonderful to have a cottage and a cow and a wife to cook your supper for you, instead of sleeping in a ditch and begging for everything. Oh, if only I was a peasant!'

Stage 4 Each group in turn reads out or improvises what it has prepared, beginning with the tramp and ending with the king. The teacher can act as narrator, joining the bits together into a complete story.

SECTION C: FREE EXPRESSION

Exercises in this section have two main purposes:
1 to give free practice in the language taught in part two section B.
2 to provide maximum opportunity for free interaction in the class.

C1 Merry-go-round

Language function: Expressing desire to do things, in writing.

Procedure
Stage 1 Prepare for writing the letter by going through and discussing the advertisement.
Stage 2 Students can write the letter individually, or in pairs or groups; it would also be suitable for a homework activity. When writing the letter they should, of course, imagine that they are living in London. It should be treated as a completely free writing activity, not tied specifically to any of the earlier exercises.

Unit 1 Part two

Stage 3 The exercise can be extended as follows: when they have finished writing the letter, students (or groups of students) exchange letters. They then reply to each other's letters with an imaginary invitation from Merry-go-round.

C2 Just the job

Language function: Imagining doing something you would like to do.

This is a *guessing game*. There is a game like this in part two section C of most units.

Procedure

Stage 1 Go through the example with the class, and ask students to guess what job they think it is about, *giving reasons* for their guess. It is important for them to identify the 'clues' in the example, since this will help them to build in clues themselves when they write the exercise.
Answer: Dentist.
It is worth pointing out the use of the conditional tense in the example to describe what a job *would* be like.

Stage 2 Divide the class into small groups. Each group *secretly* chooses a job, and constructs a short paragraph saying why they would like it, but, as in the example, without naming the job. Each group then in turn reads out its paragraph to the rest of the class, who have to guess which job is being described.
During the group writing, go from group to group giving help; at first students may find it difficult to invent 'clues' which are neither too obvious nor too obscure.

Unit 2 Excitement/Anticipation

Part one: Talking about the feeling

SECTION A: LISTENING AND DISCUSSION

 A1 Listening and **A2 Facts**

Procedure (For more detail on procedure see notes on unit 1, p. 19.)
Stage 1 Books closed. Play the dialogue once.
Stage 2 Elicit information, playing the tape again where necessary.
Stage 3 Books open. Students follow as tape is played again.
Stage 4 Facts questions are answered briefly to summarise the preceding discussion.

Answers
1 They're friends or relations.
2 They're the names of race-horses.
3 *Either* at a race-course *or* at home watching the race on TV.
4 Gladstone is winning the race.
5 To the bookmaker (or betting shop)
   He placed a bet on Gladstone and he wants to collect his winnings.
6 '... buy with all that money'
   '... do now that we're rich' etc.
7 He's suggesting that the money is *his* rather than *theirs*, since he placed the bet.

A3 Language

Procedure (For more detail on procedure see notes on unit 1, p. 21.)
Stage 1 Students answer the questions individually or in pairs.
Stage 2 Go through the answers with the whole class.

Answers
1 a   i) *They* are excit*ed*. The race is excit*ing*.
       ii) *Exciting* is not an 'absolute' adjective,

33

Unit 2 Part one

so cannot be used with 'absolutely'.
Cf. *absolutely furious* but *very/rather angry*.
(See appendix B, p. 133 for list illustrating these two points, which will recur throughout the course.)

2 b a: see no. 1 above, and appendix B.
c: *excitable* = 'likely to get excited'. It is a permanent characteristic, not a feeling.

3 a,c b and d: see no. 1 above, and appendix B.
4 a,d,e b: *self-confident* = 'sure of one's own abilities'. You cannot be 'self-confident that ...'
c = someone has assured him. This doesn't happen in the dialogue.

5 c (= are eager to) a = they *think* it will happen.
b = they can't go yet, e.g. because he is closed.

6 d to *look forward to* + noun or gerund.
7 b,c See notes on exercise B1, below.

SECTION B: PRACTICE

B1 Exciting prospects

Procedure
Stage 1 Go through the examples with the class, and discuss the differences between *excited about* and *excited at the thought/prospect of*.
You can be *excited about* i) something you *have just done* (e.g. winning the competition).
ii) something you have made *definite* arrangements to do in the future (e.g. going to Rome).
You can be *excited at the thought/prospect of* things you *imagine yourself doing* in the future (e.g. eating pizzas, visiting the Sistine Chapel).
Stage 2 Divide the class into groups or pairs, and ask them to

Unit 2 Part one

use the expressions they have learnt to talk about the feelings of the people listed. A wide range of answers is possible:
e.g. Ron is excited about being accepted by Cambridge University.
He's excited about going to Cambridge.
He's excited at the prospect of meeting a lot of new people.
He's excited at the thought of spending the afternoons boating on the river.

Stage 3 Go through the answers with the whole class.
Stage 4 Relating the language to the dialogue.
Suggested answers
Both: 'We were really excited about winning all that money.'
'We were so excited about Gladstone winning the race.'
'I was really excited at the prospect of buying a new car.'

B2 Story line

Procedure
Stage 1 Go through the example prompt and story with the class.
Stage 2 Divide the class into groups or pairs and ask them to make similar stories for the other prompts, using the expressions in italics.
Stage 3 Get the groups to read out their stories to the class.
Stage 4 Relating the language to the dialogue.
Example answer
Bill: 'Well, when we saw that Gladstone had got over the water-jump all right, we knew that he had a good chance of winning. But it wasn't until he started catching up with Evening Glow in the last two hundred metres that we really started getting excited. And he just passed her in time. We were absolutely thrilled. We couldn't wait to get down to the bookie's and collect our winnings . . . '

SECTION C: REPORTING

C1 *The list.* Get students to suggest ways in which Bill might use the listed expressions in his article.

Unit 2 Part one

Suggested answers
1 We had bet £25 on Gladstone.
2 The odds (against Gladstone winning) were 200 to 1.
3 Then he began to catch up with Evening Glow.
  We could see him catching up with Evening Glow.
4 John couldn't wait to go and collect the money.
5 I thought he was going to keep all the money for himself.
6 The turning point was at the last fence when he began to catch up.
  Winning that money was the turning point in my career.
  (= a time when a vitally important change takes place)

C2 *Reporting.* Students now write reports, either individually, in pairs or groups, or for homework. This time all the reports are from one viewpoint, Bill's, and they are written as *part of a magazine article.*

'... We were both desperate by then, so we decided to bet our last £25 on a horse called Gladstone in the 3.30 race. The odds were 200 to 1, so I didn't really think we had any chance of winning. John was confident that Gladstone could win, though – he was shouting all through the race, and getting very excited. And then, towards the end of the race, two of the leading horses fell at the water-jump, and there was only one horse, Evening Glow, in front of Gladstone. I began to feel excited myself. But it wasn't until he drew level with Evening Glow that I was sure he was going to win. And he did. Right at the last moment he put his head in front – it was the most thrilling race I've ever seen. We could hardly believe that we'd won £5,000. John couldn't wait to get down to the bookmaker and actually see the money in his hands. I remember John saying that the money was all his because he had placed the bet. He was only joking, but I believed him for a moment ...'

Unit 2 Part two

Part two: Expressing the feeling

SECTION A: RECOGNITION

A1 Breathless moments

Follow the same general procedure as for unit 1, A1 'Who wants what?' (see notes p. 25).

In this exercise the remarks are not, of course, replies, and students only have to identify the situation. However, some of the remarks could be said in a number of quite *different* situations. Get students to give as many of these alternatives as possible. Ask them to demonstrate how each remark should be said, in the situation they have chosen.

Suggested answers
1 A bird-watcher has just seen a golden eagle.
2 A football fan urging on his team during a football match. The other team has got the ball.
3 Someone watching a game of chess, advising one of the players what move to make. He is excited about the game and his friend's progress as a player.
4 Two people on a desert island waiting to be rescued. They get excited when they see a ship.
5 A politician who has just won an election, making a victory speech.
6 An anthropologist (zoologist, etc.) is examining a bone (or skull). He is excited because he thinks he may have found the remains of an early man. (Could be a detective examining a clue!)
7 Could be anybody. He is trying to solve a problem or remember a word or name.

A2 Postbag

This is a *matching exercise*. Follow the same general procedure as for unit 1, A2 'Best wishes' (see notes p. 27).

This exercise presents typical formulae used in letters to say you're looking forward to meeting someone. There are two main variables:
1 the relationship between the writer and the person receiving the letter (formal, business, intimate, etc.)
2 how strongly the feeling is expressed

37

Unit 2 Part two

Answers
1 f   2 b   3 d   4 a   5 c   6 e
Least excited: | 3 | 2/4 | 4/2 | 6 | 5 | 1 | : Most excited
Note: Numbers 2, 3 and 4 do not necessarily involve any excitement.

SECTION B: PRACTICE

Basic structures
gerunds (B1)
question forms (B2)

B1 Changes of scene

Language function: Looking forward to doing things.

Structural difficulties
1 'Look forward to' followed by noun or -ing
2 Use of negative question form *'Won't* it be . . . ' to show that you expect the other person to agree.

Procedure: Follow the same general procedure as for unit 1, B1 'Wishful thinking' (p. 28).
Stage 1   The captions for the three pictures can be *either* elicited round the class *or* worked out by the students in pairs orally or in writing.
Possible answers for picture 1
'The first thing I'm going to do when I get back is have a good meal.'
'I'm really looking forward to sleeping in a bed again.'
'I can't wait to tell my friends how I got stuck here.'
Stage 2   If necessary, give students a few minutes' preparation time for the pairwork exercise. It should be left fairly free — encourage students to have a realistic conversation rather than just produce a list of remarks as in the example.

B2 Lucky you!

Language function: Expressing excitement about what someone else is going to do.

Unit 2 Part two

Structural difficulties: Further practice of 'I wish . . . '
expressions (see unit 1, part two, B1, B3).

This exercise introduces typical social formulae for reacting to someone else's good news, and gives practice in making a single spontaneous response to a situation.

Procedure
Stage 1 Ask students to complete the remarks. Get alternatives where possible.
Stage 2 April's replies could be of two main kinds:
 i) enthusiastic agreement: e.g. 'Oh yes! I can hardly believe it's happening to me!'
 ii) deliberate understatement: e.g. 'Well, it'll make a change from Birmingham, anyway.'
Get students to suggest as many as possible.
Stage 3 A good introduction to the group activity is for the teacher to be 'April' and tell the class a piece of good news. Students react using the expressions given.
Stage 4 Divide the class into fairly large groups (at least four). The students fire remarks at 'April' in turn, and she replies to each one. When a topic is exhausted, a new 'April' takes over with a new piece of good news.

B3 Have you heard?

Language functions: Expressing excitement because something good is going to happen which will affect you; responding with indifference/suspicion.

Structural difficulties: Sequence of tenses after 'I didn't think . . . (. . . it *was* such a great achievement').

This is a *skeleton conversation*. There is an exercise like this in part two section B of most units. Students use the 'skeleton' each time, but choose between the different expressions. The parts of the conversation they produce themselves are different each time.

Procedure
Stage 1 Ask students to complete Jack's and Jill's remarks, giving alternatives where possible. Remind them that Jack is *excited*, and Jill is *indifferent* at first.
Possible answers
Jack: Have you heard the news? *There's a new super-sonic airliner which gets to New York in half the normal time!*

Unit 2 Part two

>Jill: Yes, I read about it. I didn't think *it was such a great achievement.*
>Jack: But just imagine! People will be able to *get to New York in 3 hours!*
>Jill: Yes, but *you can* already *get there quickly enough, can't you?*
>Jack: But don't you see? It'll mean that *you can go to America for lunch and come back to London in time for dinner.*
>Jill: Hmm, yes. I suppose *that would be quite exciting.*
>Jack: Exactly! And what's more, *it'll make things much easier for businessmen.*
>Jill: Hmm, yes. You could be right. Maybe *it's quite a good idea after all.*

Stage 2 After establishing how the remarks could continue, students act out the conversation in pairs, choosing only *one* of the alternatives.

Stage 3 Prepare for the improvisation by discussing:
a) what the headlines are about
b) why Jack might be excited (i.e. what good effects the innovations might have).

Stage 4 Divide the class into pairs. The students improvise the three conversations, using the 'skeleton'.

SECTION C: FREE EXPRESSION

C1 Old and new

Language functions: Expressing excitement because something good is going to happen which will affect you; reacting with indifference or suspicion.

This exercise gives further practice of the language introduced in B3 above. The exercise is a *half-and-half improvisation*. There is an exercise like this in part two section C of most units.

Procedure: This exercise has two distinct stages: a *preparation stage* and an *interaction stage*.

Stage 1 Preparation
Divide the class into pairs. Give roles to each *pair*, alternately, so that half the pairs are *both* Freda, and the other half are *both* Mrs Mullet. Together, pairs study the instructions for their role and think of some

of the things they might say. They should *not* try to write their part of the conversation, but may make very brief notes.

Stage 2 Interaction
Students form new pairs, so that each pair consists of one Freda and one Mrs Mullet. This can be done very simply by each student turning to face the student on the other side of him. They then improvise the conversation.

This activity works best with an even number of students. If you have an odd number in your class, form one group of three. Two of the students in this group stay together for the whole activity, i.e. behave as if they are one person.

If there is time, it is worthwhile forming new pairs again as the improvisation begins to peter out. Students then improvise the conversation a second time, but with different partners.

C2 What's new?

Language function: Being excited (in writing) because you have just had an exciting idea.

This is a *guessing game*. For general procedure see notes on unit 1, C2 'Just the job' (p. 32).

The letter-writer has just invented the wheel.
Students form groups, secretly choose an invention, and write a similar letter. These are then read out, and other groups guess what the invention is.

Unit 3 Worry/Apprehension

Part one: Talking about the feeling

SECTION A: LISTENING AND DISCUSSION

A1 Listening and **A2 Facts**

Procedure (For more detail on procedure see notes on unit 1, p. 19.)
Stage 1 Books closed. Play the dialogue once.
Stage 2 Elicit information, playing the tape again where necessary.
Stage 3 Books open. Students follow as tape is played again.
Stage 4 'Facts' questions are answered briefly to summarise the preceding discussion.

Answers
1 He's the local policeman.
2 Probably at the police station.
3 Mrs Ponsonby's pet, e.g. dog or cat. (*'Answers to the name of Augustus'*)
4 Augustus disappeared.
5 '. . . left the door open'
   '. . . been so unkind to him'
   '. . . taken him out without a lead', etc.
6 He's preparing to take some notes (picking up a pencil, opening his book, etc.).

A3 Language

Procedure (For more detail on procedure see notes on unit 1, p. 21.)
Stage 1 Students answer the questions individually or in pairs.
Stage 2 Go through the answers with the whole class.

Answers
1 a,e See B1 'Strength of feeling' and B2 'Shades of meaning' below.
2 a   b and c = *involved in* or *connected with*.

42

Unit 3 Part one

	For a, see B2 'Shades of meaning' below.
3 b,c	You can be *wild with* excitement, joy, etc., not with worry.
4 c (= to stop her worrying)	a = to give her an insurance policy. b 'to assure someone *that* . . . ' = 'to say confidently that . . . '.
5 b	a: see no. 4 a above. c: see no. 4 c above.

SECTION B: PRACTICE

B1 Strength of feeling

Procedure
Stage 1 Go through the example paragraph with the class.
Stage 2 Discuss the differences in meaning between the four adjectives:
frightened = afraid, scared
nervous = a little bit frightened (as before an exam)
terrified = very frightened
apprehensive = you have a feeling that something bad is going to happen in the future. You're not *necessarily* afraid — e.g. question (e) below.
Students will find it easier to show these differences by way of examples than by attempting to define them.
Note: Point out that *nervous* does *not* mean *angry* or *irritated*, as its equivalent does in many languages.
Stage 3 In groups or pairs, students decide how they would feel in the five situations given.
Suggested answers
a) nervous   b) apprehensive   c) nervous
d) frightened/terrified   e) apprehensive

B2 Shades of meaning

1 Go through the introduction and examples with the class.
2 In groups or pairs, students construct appropriate sentences using the information from the table.
Example answers
Mr Green is worried about going back to work.
Mrs Green is anxious about her husband's health.

Unit 3 Part one

The doctor is concerned about the success of the operation.
Mr Green's workmates are concerned about his health.
Mr Green is worried about losing his job.
Mr Green is anxious in case he loses his job.
3 Go through the answers together.

B3 Story line

Stage 1 Go through the example reports with the class. Make sure the students understand the language points and the situation.
Stage 2 In groups or pairs, students construct two further reports for each of the three situations given (or different groups can be assigned different situations). Note that students must deduce what the person is worried about from the direct language:
1 Mr Matthews has some symptoms which are common in middle or old age, e.g. shortness of breath, pains in the joints, nervous trouble, etc.
2 Mrs Nelson is worried about her teenage son who is off doing something she thinks is dangerous e.g. mountain climbing, pot-holing.
3 Anthony has got a university degree in Latin, and is worried in case he won't be able to find a job.
Stage 3 Go through students' answers with the whole class.
Stage 4 Relating the language to the dialogue:
Mrs Ponsonby: 'I was out of my mind with worry about poor Augustus. But the policeman really cheered me up and told me he'd turn up soon.'
Mr Steadman: 'Poor Mrs Ponsonby was so worried about her dog. She wouldn't stop talking about it. I tried to reassure her and I took some notes. She soon cheered up.'

SECTION C: REPORTING

C1 *The list.* Get students to suggest ways in which either Mrs Ponsonby or Mr Steadman might use the listed expressions to tell the story of what happened.

Suggested answers
1 Mr Steadman: 'She seemed terribly upset about what had happened.'

Unit 3 Part one

2 Mr Steadman: 'She was afraid she'd never see her dog again.'
3 Mr Steadman: 'I was afraid she'd burst into tears.'
4 Mr Steadman: 'She kept blaming herself.'
5 Mr Steadman: 'She felt that she was to blame.'
6 Mr Steadman: 'She obviously felt very guilty about it.'
7 Mr Steadman: 'I sat and listened as patiently as I could.'
8 Mr Steadman: 'I did my best to calm her down.'
9 Mr Steadman: 'I took down the details.'

Mrs Ponsonby could use any of the same expressions in roughly the same way, e.g. 'I was so upset about what had happened', etc.

C2 *Reporting.* Students now write reports, either individually, in pairs or groups, or for homework. Approximately half the reports should be from Mrs Ponsonby's point of view, and half from Mr Steadman's point of view.

Two possible reports

Mrs Ponsonby: '... Well, my dear, when three days had gone by and he still hadn't come back, I was almost out of my mind with worry — I was so afraid he might have had an accident or been stolen or something. Anyway, I went down to the police station, and told them all about it. There was an awfully nice young man there — he listened very patiently while I told him what had happened and then he took down all the details in a big green book. He really was a great help, and he seemed so sure that they'd find my poor little Augustus that I immediately felt a lot better. *Such* a nice young man, he was ... '

Mr Steadman: '... Mrs Ponsonby was in today. She'd lost that dog of hers again. She was so upset about it, I could hardly get her to give me the details. She obviously felt very guilty about it — she kept blaming herself for what had happened. Anyway, I tried to reassure her as much as I could, and eventually managed to put her mind at rest. Poor old Mrs Ponsonby. I wonder why it keeps running away like that ... '

Unit 3 Part two

Part two: Expressing the feeling

SECTION A: RECOGNITION

A1 A bundle of nerves

Follow the same general procedure as for unit 1, A1 'Who wants what?' (see notes, p. 25).

Suggested answers
1 Two people are crossing a field. One of them is worried because the 'cows' in the field look rather aggressive, and she thinks they may be bulls.
2 Someone has to do something at 7 o'clock that he feels nervous about, e.g. a date, an interview, a performance, going into battle.
3 Mrs Hansford has answered the telephone. On the other end is a stranger with a sinister voice. She's frightened.
4 Two people, possibly alone in an old house, hear a strange noise. One of them is frightened. The other tries to reassure him, but begins to get frightened himself.
5 Nervous passenger in a car, speaking to the driver, who has just taken a corner too fast. She is trying not to show her nervousness too much.
6 It's late at night. A heavy smoker has just discovered that there are no cigarettes left.
7 Someone adding up how much she's spent, and finding that it's more than she thought.

A2 Lost in the post

Note: The recording gives the answers: use only at the round-up stage.

This is a *matching exercise*. Follow the same general procedure as for unit 1, A2 'Best wishes' (see notes, p. 27).

This exercise presents typical expressions for expressing worry, and for reassuring someone who is worried. The 'worried' expressions show different strengths of feeling, from slightly worried to desperate.

Answers
George: D B E   A (or C)   C (or A)
Room-mate: C A D (or E) E (or D)   B

46

Unit 3 Part two

SECTION B: PRACTICE

> Basic structures
> 1st conditional (B1)
> indirect questions (B1)
> *might/could* + *have done* (B2)
> gerunds (B3)

B1 Alarming thoughts

Language function: Worrying about possible consequences, either 'thinking aloud' or shared worry.

Structural difficulties
1 Use of present simple after 'I hope', 'What if' and 'Supposing', to refer to the future.
2 Use of 'what if' and 'supposing'. These mean the same, and are used to talk about *unpleasant* possibilities:
   e.g. '*I hope* I find it.'   '*What if* I don't find it?'
         '*I hope* I haven't lost it.'   '*Supposing* I've lost it?'

Procedure: Follow the same general procedure as for unit 1, B1 'Wishful thinking' (see notes, p. 28).

The pairwork conversation might go something like this:

A: Mm. Ten past ten. I wonder where he's got to.
B: Yes. Supposing he's lost the address?
A: I hope not. Anyway, if he doesn't get here by half past, we'll have to give him up.
B: Oh dear. I hope he comes. Otherwise we'll have to . . .

The conversation should be left fairly free. If you like, ask each pair at the end what solutions (if any) they found to their problems.

B2 Far from home

Language functions: Expressing anxiety about somebody else; reassuring someone who is anxious.

Structural difficulties
1 Use of *what if/supposing* + present perfect, to talk about unpleasant things that might have happened.

Unit 3 Part two

2 Use of *might/could* + have done, for speculating about the past.

Procedure

Stage 1 Go through the example, which is one half of a dialogue, with Peter's father's replies missing. Ask students to suggest the father's replies.
Possible answers
'There's nothing to worry about.'
'Nonsense. He can't have done.'
'Don't be ridiculous – there aren't any bears in the Lake District.'
'I'm sure he can look after himself.'

Stage 2 Divide the class into pairs. Each pair acts out the conversation between Peter's mother and father. They then have similar conversations based on the three other topics, changing roles each time.

B3 Cold feet

Language function: Expressing apprehension about your own future.

Structural difficulties: None.

This is a *skeleton conversation*. Follow the same general procedure as for unit 2, B3 'Have you heard?' (see notes, p. 39).

This skeleton conversation is rather freer – the expressions given form only the opening of the conversation, which students continue in any way they like. A possible development:

Malcolm: Oh, it's just the thought of spending the whole day with a crowd of noisy children.
Janet: Oh, I see.
Malcolm: You see, the trouble is that I don't really like children. I've never managed to find anything to say to them.
Janet: Well, in that case, why are you going to be a teacher?
Malcolm: Well, you see, I've got a degree in Latin, and ...

SECTION C: FREE EXPRESSION

C1 Psychiatrist's couch

Language functions: Expressing extreme anxiety about yourself,

Unit 3 Part two

and explaining your personal problems; reassuring someone who is worried, and giving helpful advice.

This is a *half-and-half improvisation*. Follow the same general procedure as for unit 2, C1 'Old and new' (see notes, p. 40). Prepare for the exercise by discussing the notes from the psychiatrist's interview with Andrew's parents. Discuss especially:
1 *Why* Andrew might be the way he is.
2 To what extent his parents' opinion is to be trusted.
Do not, however, discuss what might be said in the interview between the psychiatrist and Andrew, which should be left for the *preparation stage*, in pairs.

C2 What's up?

Language functions: Expressing anxiety in a letter; writing about personal problems.

This is a *guessing game*. Follow the same general procedure as for unit 1, C2 (see notes, p. 32). Point out to the class that they do not have to write a *complete* letter — a paragraph from the beginning or middle would be enough.

Unit 4 Admiration

Part one: Talking about the feeling

SECTION A: LISTENING AND DISCUSSION

A1 Listening and **A2** Facts

Procedure (For more detail on procedure see notes on unit 1, p. 19.)
Stage 1 Books closed. Play tape of dialogue once.
Stage 2 Elicit information, playing tape again where necessary.
Stage 3 Books open. Students follow as tape is played again.
Stage 4 'Facts' questions are discussed briefly to summarise the preceding discussion.

Answers
1 Acquaintances or distant relatives.
2 At George's house.
3 He's looking at it, turning it over in his hands, etc.
4 'Elegant' refers mainly to the shape and style of the vase, 'dignified' refers mainly to its age and size, i.e. the vase is big, old and has a pleasing shape.
5 He doesn't like it.
6 He probably thinks that Clarence has bad taste, or that he's crazy.
7 Clarence probably thinks the same about George.

A3 Language

Procedure (For more detail on procedure see notes on unit 1, p. 21.)
Stage 1 Students answer the questions individually or in pairs.
Stage 2 Go through the answers with the whole class.

Answers
1 a,c   d: possible but rather strong.
        b = emotionally affected.
        See B1 'First impressions', below.

Unit 4 Part one

2 c,d   a,b: he could only *praise* the vase if George had made it himself.
        e,f: you can only *compliment* and *congratulate* people. See B2 'Words of praise', below.
3 b,c   a is too weak.
        d,e are too strong.
        See unit 1, B1 'Strength of feeling' (p. 22).
4 b   a is used for *moral* attitudes.
        c = to make a rough calculation.
5 d   a,b = to *escape from*, e.g. a trap.
        c is old-fashioned, and would only be used very formally.
6 b,c,d The usage of *offer*:
        'Have a cigarette' — He *offered me* a cigarette.
        'I'll carry it for you' — He *offered to* carry it for me.
        'You can drive if you like' — He *offered to let me* drive.
7 a (= he likes them)   b would be correct in a phrase like 'he's
   c (= he knows a lot   an amateur antiques collector' (i.e. not
      about them)   professional).

SECTION B: PRACTICE

B1   **First impressions**

Procedure
Stage 1 Go through the examples with the class. Bring students' attention to the two alternative structures presented.
Stage 2 Discuss the differences in meaning between the four adjectives:
        You're *impressed* — you think something is good or done well (e.g. efficient service, a fine building)
        You're *struck* — something unusual catches your attention and you like it (e.g. waiters' costumes, an unusual work of art)
        You're *moved* — something affects you emotionally, so that you want to cry (e.g. beautiful music, an eloquent speech)
        You're *overwhelmed* — you're so *impressed* or *moved* that you don't know what to say.
        Students will find it easier to show these differences by way of examples than by attempting to define them.
        Note: quite used with *striking* = *rather* (cf. *quite good*);

Unit 4 Part one

> *quite* used with *overwhelmingly* = *completely*, *absolutely* (cf. *quite finished*).

Stage 3 In groups or pairs, students talk about Françoise's feelings using the seven extracts from her postcards. Make sure they use both structures in their answers.
Suggested answers
a) impressed   b) overwhelmed or impressed
c) struck   d) moved or overwhelmed   e) overwhelmed or impressed   f) struck or impressed
g) moved or overwhelmed

B2 Words of praise

Procedure
Stage 1 Go through the examples with the class.
Stage 2 In groups or pairs, students use appropriate expressions to describe the reactions of the guests to the things that happened at the party. There are several possible answers to each question.
Suggested answers
1 They *congratulated me on* getting a new job.
2 They *admired/were full of admiration for/complimented her on* her dress.
3 They *praised/were full of praise for/complimented me on* the meal/my cooking.
4 They *admired/were full of admiration for* the garden, flowers, etc.
5 They *praised/were full of praise for* her performance/playing/skill, etc.
6 They *complimented me on* my choice of wine.
They *praised/were full of praise for* the wine (wine = an achievement on the part of the people who made it).
7 They *admired/were full of admiration for* the aeroplanes.
They *praised/were full of praise for* his workmanship.
Stage 4 Relating the language to the dialogue:
George: 'Clarence *admired/was full of admiration for* the vase.'

SECTION C: REPORTING

C1 *The list*. Get students to suggest ways in which either Clarence

Unit 4 Part one

or George might use the listed expressions to tell the story of what happened.
Suggested answers
1 Clarence: 'I suddenly noticed a beautiful vase . . . '
  George: 'He suddenly noticed an old vase . . . '
2 Clarence: 'To my surprise he offered to give it to me.'
  George: 'To my surprise he seemed to like it very much.'
3 Clarence: 'He didn't seem to realise its value.'
  George: 'I could see that it was of great value.'
4 Clarence: 'Of course I accepted it.'
  George: 'He accepted it immediately.'
5 Clarence: 'I was absolutely delighted to have it.'
  George: 'He seemed delighted to get it.'
6 Clarence: 'He obviously didn't appreciate it/its beauty.'

C2 *Reporting*. Students now write reports, either individually, in pairs or groups, or for homework. Approximately half the reports should be from Clarence's point of view, and half from George's point of view.

Two possible reports
Clarence: ' . . . We were sitting in his lounge when I suddenly noticed an exceptionally beautiful late-Victorian vase that was standing half-hidden on the sideboard; I was really quite struck by its elegance. To my surprise, when I asked him about it he didn't seem interested. He obviously didn't realise its value, because as soon as I started admiring it, he offered to give it to me. Of course I accepted it, although I did feel a bit guilty about just taking it without offering him any money. Still, if he can't appreciate works of art, that's his problem. Poor old George . . . '
George: ' . . . As soon as Clarence came into the lounge, he started looking at all the ornaments and commenting on them — you know the way he likes to pretend he's a great connoisseur of antiques. Anyway, he suddenly noticed an old vase we have on the sideboard — a hideous Victorian thing that Mother found in the attic, and refuses to throw away. But Clarence seemed to think it was marvellous — he picked it up and started admiring it, and it was obvious he was hoping I'd give it to him. Well, I thought if he was so eager to have a piece of rubbish like that, I'd let him have it — so I did. Actually, I was glad to get rid of it. And he was delighted! Poor old Clarence . . . '

Unit 4 Part two

Part two: Expressing the feeling

SECTION A: RECOGNITION

A1 Good for you

Follow the same general procedure as for unit 1, A1 ('Who wants what?' (see notes, p. 25).
In this exercise, students should pay particular attention to the *relationship* between the speaker and the listener (e.g. superior to inferior, members of the same family, instructor to pupil, etc.).

Suggested answers
1 Friends or family talking to someone who has just given some public performance, e.g. sports day, school play, concert, etc.
2 Two friends, one of whom has just completed a piece of work with his/her hands, e.g. embroidery.
3 Friend to schoolteacher, busy mother, friend with noisy neighbours, etc.
4 A fan to some famous person connected with the Arts — sculptor, writer, etc. This is the first time they have met, and could be at an exhibition or party.
5 Written greeting on a card or present from child to mother.
6 Instructor, teacher or casual observer to someone who's learning how to do something, e.g. swim.
7 Teacher's written comment at the end of a student's composition.
8 Someone playing with a baby, pet, etc. — at any rate, something that is alive, small, pretty and can't talk.

A2 Put in a good word

This exercise gives insight into the use of 'superlatives' for expressing admiration. Point out to the class:
1 There are two kinds of 'superlative' in English (as in other languages): those that have a fairly precise meaning (like the six listed in the exercise), and those which are so widely used that they have lost their original meaning (like *fantastic*).
2 Superlatives (of either kind) *cannot* be qualified by *very*; instead they are used with *absolutely*, *really* or *quite* (meaning *completely*).
3 Superlatives of the 'meaningless' kind are usually considered

Unit 4 Part two

slang. They go in and out of fashion, and often vary from one generation, social group, etc., to another.

Answers
1 delicious   2 delightful (charming)   3 charming (delightful)   4 unforgettable   5 brilliant   6 ideal
Words like 'fantastic': *great, fabulous*, splendid, marvellous, *wonderful, amazing, incredible*, tremendous, remarkable, magnificent, superb, terrific, lovely, etc.
(The words in italics in the list are used especially by younger people.)

SECTION B: PRACTICE

Basic structures
tag questions (B1)
infinitives and gerunds (B2, B3)

B1   Introvert Irene and extrovert Ernie

Language function: Admiring something you see.

Structural difficulties: Use of *'What a* + adjective + noun' to express admiration (cf. *'How* + adjective').

This exercise presents and practises typical expressions used for admiring things, either mildly or strongly according to the kind of person you are.

Procedure
Stage 1   Ask students to point out the differences between Irene's language and Ernie's language, and build up two lists:
Irene
'modified' expressions (not bad, quite, rather)
tag questions (isn't it? Don't you?)
Ernie
superlatives (amazing, brilliant, etc.)
Isn't it . . . ! What a . . . ! How . . . !
'Emphatic' forms (I *do* think . . .)
Stage 2   Divide the class into pairs. Give them roles (Irene or Ernie), which they change half way through the exer-

55

Unit 4 Part two

cise. They make random comments about each of the things in the photographs, developing them into a conversation if they wish, but always using language appropriate to their role.

B2   How do you do it?

Language functions: Admiring someone to his/her face; replying modestly to compliments.

Structural difficulties
Use of *the way* as a sentence connective. This is very common in English, and can be used in two ways:
1 meaning literally *the manner* in which someone does something
   e.g. 'I like the way you dance.'
2 *not* meaning literally *the manner*, but rather *the fact that* someone does something:
   e.g. 'I admire the way you keep your house so clean.'
   (= You keep your house so clean. I admire that.)
The way can be used in the same sense after other verbs, e.g. love, like, hate, object to, resent.

Procedure
Follow the same general procedure as for unit 2, B2 'Lucky you' (see notes, p. 38).
Stage 1   a) Things Mrs Brown can do better:
Cope with her job, keep the house clean, find time for the children, go out in the evening, keep looking young, etc.
b) Admiring remarks:
'How do you manage to keep looking so young?'
'I do admire the way you keep the house so clean.'
'I wish I could rush around without getting tired the way you do.'
'I do envy you. You seem to have time for everything.'
'You're so good at making bread, too!'
'I think the way you get so much typing done is absolutely amazing!'
c) Modest replies:
'Oh, there's nothing to it really.'
'Don't exaggerate – it's not very difficult.'
'Well, I like to be active, you know.'
Stage 2   Divide the class into groups of at least four. The student

Unit 4 Part two

being admired should make a suitable reply to each remark addressed to him.

B3 Cheering news

Language functions: Expressing approval of something you hear about, disagreeing and arguing.

Structural difficulties: None.

This is a *skeleton conversation*. Follow the same general procedure as for unit 2, B3 'Have you heard?' (see notes, p. 39). This exercise introduces formulae for expressing approval, and is 'open-ended', i.e. it can continue as a free argument.

Stage 1 Possible answers
  a) Smith: Put a tax on cigarettes; tax luxuries; encourage people to give up smoking; discourage smoking.
  b) Jones: But they could have done it more gradually. But there was no need to put it up quite so much.

Stage 2 Prepare for the pairwork by discussing what the newspaper headlines mean, and what are the arguments for and against in each case.

Stage 3 Students improvise further conversations in pairs, changing roles for each conversation.

SECTION C: FREE EXPRESSION

C1 Between friends

Language functions: Complimenting and/or admiring someone in order to cheer them up.

This is a *half-and-half improvisation*. Follow the same general procedure as for unit 2, C1 'Old and new' (see notes, p. 40).

C2 Who's who?

Language functions: Admiring a person and his/her achievements, to his/her face.

This is a *guessing game*. Follow the same general procedure as for unit 1, C2 'Just the job' (see notes, p. 32).

Unit 4 Part two

Stage 1 Students guess who is being admired in the example.
Answer: Leonardo da Vinci (being admired by the husband of Mona Lisa, who commissioned him to paint her).
Stage 2 Students form groups, secretly choose a famous person and write a paragraph admiring him/her to his/her face.
Stage 3 Groups read their paragraphs aloud, and other groups guess who is being admired.

Unit 5 Irritation/Impatience

Part one: Talking about the feeling

SECTION A: LISTENING AND DISCUSSION

A1 Listening and **A2 Facts**

Procedure (For more detail on procedure see notes on unit 1, p. 19.)
Stage 1   Books closed. Play the dialogue once.
Stage 2   Elicit information, playing the tape again where necessary.
Stage 3   Books open. Students follow as tape is played again.
Stage 4   Facts questions are answered briefly to summarise the preceding discussion.

Answers
1 In a shared room or flat, probably on a university campus.
2 They're probably students. They're room-mates or flat-mates.
3 She is tapping a pencil, pen, fingers, etc. on the table.
4 She is trying to read, study, etc.
5 She wants her to stop tapping.
6 She ignores Sue. She keeps on tapping.
7 She walks out of the room, slams the door and goes to the library.

A3 Language

Procedure (For more detail on procedure see notes on unit 1, p. 21.)
Stage 1   Students answer the questions individually or in pairs.
Stage 2   Go through the answers with the whole class.

Answers
1 b,e   a = a little frightened.
           c is possible, but a little strong.
           See B1 'Most annoying', below.
2 c   'Irritable' describes a general characteristic.

Unit 5 Part one

An irritable person is one who easily gets irritated. Cf. bad-tempered.
3 b   c: you distract *someone* (see no. 4, below).
a: you *draw* someone's attention *to* something; to attract someone's attention = to draw his attention to yourself.
4 a,c   to distract = to stop someone concentrating.
to disturb = to annoy someone by breaking into what he's doing (e.g. 'Do not disturb' notice on hotel room door).
b = to break into a conversation or somebody's work suddenly, by talking to him.
5 b   The others are too loud.
6 a,b,c   d = doesn't see.
7 a,c,d   a is very colloquial.
b: 'Carry' would have a literal meaning here (e.g. a heavy suitcase).

SECTION B: PRACTICE

B1 **Most annoying**

Stage 1   Go through the example with the class.
Stage 2   Discuss the differences in meaning between the three adjectives.
If you're *impatient*, you're tired of waiting for something or to do something.
If you're *irritated* or *annoyed*, you're a little bit angry. Both words can be used of:
i) single actions, e.g. 'The remark irritated/annoyed him.'
ii) repeated actions, e.g. 'I was irritated/annoyed by the way he kept blowing his nose.'
(For *annoyed*, see also unit 7, B1 'Bad feeling', p. 77.)
Stage 3   Students use the expressions given to talk about Alan and Alice.
Suggested answers
a) Alan is impatient to go out.
Alan is getting impatient with Alice.
b) annoyed/irritated
c) impatient and annoyed/irritated
d) impatient and annoyed/irritated
e) annoyed/irritated
f) impatient

Unit 5 Part one

B2 Story line

For general procedure, see notes for unit 1, B2 'Story line' p. 22).
Stage 1 Go through introduction and example with the class.
Stage 2 In groups or pairs, students construct similar paragraphs for the five prompts given. This exercise is freer than previous 'story line' exercises, in that the language they use to 'set the scene' for each situation is not controlled.
Stage 3 Go through the answers with the whole class.
Stage 4 Relating the language to the dialogue:
Sue: 'My room-mate's so inconsiderate. I was sitting trying to study for my exam this morning, and she was tapping her pen on the table, so I couldn't concentrate. I asked her to stop, but she didn't take any notice of me. She just carried on tapping.'

SECTION C: REPORTING

C1 *The list.* Get students to suggest ways in which Sue might use the listed expressions to talk about what happened.

Suggested answers

'I got (really) fed up with my room-mate.' (= tired of, irritated with)

'She really got on my nerves.' (= irritated me. Note that we can use *nerves* in this way, but not *nervous*.)

'I was trying to/couldn't concentrate on my book.'
'She disturbed/was disturbing/kept disturbing me.'
'She prevented me from reading/doing my work, etc.'
'In the end/Eventually I decided to go and work in the library.' (*Finally* could also be used here but not *At last* (which = after waiting for something for a long time, e.g. 'At last the letter arrived').)

C2 *Reporting.* Students now write reports, either individually, in pairs or groups, or for homework. This time the reports are all from Sue's point of view.

Possible report
'That room-mate of mine! She really gets on my nerves! I don't know what was the matter with her yesterday afternoon — I suppose she had nothing to do. She just sat there tapping her pen on the table while I was trying to study. Naturally, I began to get irritated, because I couldn't concentrate on my book. It was so inconsiderate. I asked her to stop several times, but she didn't take the slightest bit of notice; she just kept on tapping. Well, in the end, I couldn't stand it any longer, and I had to go and work in the library. I was so annoyed I slammed the door as hard as I could. I think I'll have to start looking for a new room-mate.'

Part two: Expressing the feeling

SECTION A: RECOGNITION

A1 Sweet or sour?

Follow the same general procedure as for unit 1, A1 'Who wants what?' (see notes, p. 25).
As suggested by the title, not all the remarks *necessarily* show impatience or irritation (numbers 4 and 7). During the round-up, it is worth asking students to demonstrate how they would say the remark. This can then be compared with the version on the tape.

Suggested answers
1 B keeps asking A the time (of a TV programme, train departure, etc.) and A, answering for the third time, is getting irritated. It is *not* a football score, which would be 'five four', without the 'to'.
2 Either an impatient passenger to a slow driver, or a cautious passenger to a driver eager to overtake. Could be a spectator at a race.
3 A reply to someone who is over-eager to help in giving directions, or who is insisting on taking someone home (e.g. after a party).
4 An English teacher correcting a student.

Unit 5 Part two

5 Someone who is unable to untie a knot, parcel, etc. He is irritated with the thing, not with the other person.
6 Wife/girlfriend to jealous husband/boyfriend (or the other way round), who keeps asking the same old question.
7 Someone is upstairs, and has just been called.
8 Probably boyfriend to girlfriend who wants to go home early, after some argument.

A2 Waiting list

This is a *matching exercise*. Follow the same general procedure as for unit 1, A2 'Best wishes' (see notes, p. 27).

This exercise presents typical expressions for showing impatience without giving offence. There are two main variables.
1 degree of formality (only the informal expressions *openly* show impatience).
2 whether you are getting someone to *do* something or asking for information.

Answers
a) 2,3,5 (all used to get someone to do something, formal)
b) 1,6,8 (all used to get information, formal)
c) Especially 4,7,9 (all informal), but any of the nine expressions is possible. It is worth discussing what differences (e.g. in your relationship with your friend) would lead to different expressions being used.

Note: 2 and 5 could be used for (b) if followed by 'tell me'.

At the end of the exercise, ask students to complete each of the utterances.

Although this exercise is intended for recognition only, it could be extended with a short practice stage, in which students have short conversations (in pairs) for each of the three situations.

SECTION B: PRACTICE

> *Basic structures*
> tag questions (B2)
> *I wish* + *would* (B1, B2, B3)
> indirect questions (B2)
> 2nd conditional (B3)

Unit 5 Part two

B1 Victimisation

Language function: Expressing irritation in an informal situation to stop someone doing something.

Structural difficulties
1 More practice of *I wish* + *would* (see unit 1).
2 Use of tags, *will you?* and *can't you?* after imperative sentences, to make irritated requests.

Procedure
Stage 1 Point out that the relationship between the people in the example is *very* informal, and that the expressions practised in this exercise should only be used with friends!
Stage 2 After going through the examples, go through the list of 'irritating actions', to make sure the class understands what they mean.
Stage 3 A good introduction to the exercise is for the *teacher* to do the things in the list (in any order), and to continue until someone in the class makes him stop by using one of the expressions from the example.
Stage 4 Divide the class into groups of at least four. In turns, individual students *do* the things in the list (in any order). The other students fire irritated requests at him to make him stop.

B2 Wishful thinking

Language function: 'Shared' impatience, i.e. two people both express impatience for something to happen.

Structural difficulties
1 Use of *It's about time* + past tense to show impatience (cf. *It's time*; *It's high time*).
   e.g. 'It's time for the bus to arrive.' = the bus is due now.
   'It's time the bus came.' = the bus is late.
2 Use of *ought to* + *have done* for talking about things that haven't happened.

Procedure
Stage 1 Go through the expressions with the class, asking students to complete them. Divide the class into pairs. Students improvise two-line conversations like those in the pictures. Each of the expressions can be used in either the opening remark or the reply.

Unit 5 Part two

Stage 2 Students improvise similar two-line conversations for the other situations. Insist that they use different structures from the list each time, so that they practise the whole range of expressions.

B3 Beauty and the Beasts

Language functions: Showing increasing annoyance in a formal situation (disguised at first, but becoming more open); making excuses; persuading someone to do something.

Structural difficulties: None.

This is a *skeleton conversation*. Follow the same general procedure as for unit 2, B3 'Have you heard?' (see notes, p. 39).

Possible version of the conversation
Beast: Would you like me to get you a drink?
Beauty: No thanks. I've just had one.
Beast: Well, why don't you have another?
Beauty: No, honestly, I don't feel like a drink at the moment.
Beast: Oh, come on. Another one won't do you any harm. What shall I get you? Whisky?
Beauty: Look. I've told you twice already — I don't want a drink!
Beast: How about a glass of wine, then?
Beauty: Really! I do wish you'd stop bothering me!

During the further practice, with Beasts 2, 3 and 4, students should be able to make up Beast's remarks and Beauty's excuses *as they go along*. A good way to round up this exercise is to get students to report briefly how their conversations developed.

SECTION C: FREE EXPRESSION

C1 Delaying tactics

Language function: Showing impatience in a formal situation without giving offence.

This is a *half-and-half improvisation*. Follow the same general procedure as for unit 2, C1 'Old and new' (see notes, p. 40). The easiest way to conduct this exercise is for the whole class to choose the same situation (whichever one is closest to their own experience).

Unit 5 Part two

Afterwards, the exercise can be repeated with a second situation, with all those who were student A becoming student B. In this way every student practises getting irritated *and* making excuses.

C2 Do not disturb

Language functions: Asking persistent questions; showing increasing irritation in an informal situation.

This is a *guessing game*. Follow the same general procedure as for unit 1, C2 'Just the job' (see notes, p. 32). In this exercise, the guessing is done from a dialogue, which each group/pair either writes and then acts out, or prepares and then improvises in front of the class.

Answer to the example situation: Kojak
(If your students are unlikely to be familiar with Kojak, construct your own example dialogue around a programme that is currently popular.)

Unit 6 Delight/Relief

Part one: Talking about the feeling

SECTION A: LISTENING AND DISCUSSION

A1 Listening and **A2** Facts

Procedure (For more detail on procedure see notes on unit 1, p. 19.)
Stage 1 Books closed. Play the dialogue once.
Stage 2 Elicit information, playing the tape again where necessary.
Stage 3 Books open. Students follow as tape is played again.
Stage 4 Facts questions are answered briefly to summarise the preceding discussion.

Answers
1 Friends, probably close friends (on the surface, anyway).
2 '... would like to come with us.'
3 Because she doesn't want to go on holiday with Maisy and her husband, and she wants to avoid any embarrassment.
4 She probably hasn't got any.
5 She offers her the house.
  She offers to let her stay in the house.
  (For *offer* see notes on unit 4, A3 'Language', no. 6 (p. 51))
6 i) because they will not be using it themselves.
  ii) because she wants Tony to look after the garden.

A3 Language

Procedure (For more detail on procedure see notes on unit 1, p. 21.)
Stage 1 Students answer the questions individually or in pairs.
Stage 2 Go through the answers with the whole class.

Answers
1 b   a = she waits for something to happen.
      c = she has been talking and she stops.

67

Unit 6 Part one

2 a,c *engagement* = a particular appointment, e.g. 'I have an engagement on Thursday.'
3 a,b,c c is all right, but rather strong.
d,e: these are too weak, and are not 'absolute' adjectives, so cannot be used after 'absolutely'.
4 a,d b,c,e: 'absolute' adjectives cannot be used with 'very'.
5 b,c,d a: you are glad *about* something. For meaning differences see B1 'Good news', below.

SECTION B: PRACTICE

B1 Good news

Stage 1 Go through the example situation with the class.
Stage 2 Discuss how the three people feel:
They are all *glad* or *pleased*.
Jack, in particular, is *delighted*.
Jill, in particular, is *relieved*.
Stage 3 In groups or pairs, students talk about the feelings of the six people in the exercise, using complete sentences as in the examples.
Answers
1 glad/pleased
2 relieved (delighted)
3 relieved
4 delighted
5 glad/pleased
6 relieved (delighted)
Stage 4 Relating the language to the dialogue.
See A3 'Language' questions 3, 4 and 5. Also:
Clare: 'I am relieved that Maisy didn't ask us to go to Nice with them.'

B2 Story line

Stage 1 Go through the examples with the class. Note that the reports are from two points of view.
Stage 2 In groups or pairs, students construct similar reports for the three situations given. In each case, they must decide what the person concerned was afraid *might* happen.
Stage 3 Go through the answers with the whole class.
Stage 4 Relating the language to the dialogue:

Clare: 'For a moment I was afraid she was going to ask us to go to Nice with them. But as it turned out she wanted to offer us her house for the summer. Of course, I was absolutely delighted ... '

Maisy: 'She looked rather embarrassed when I mentioned Nice. She must have thought I was going to invite them to come with us. Of course, when I offered her the house, she was absolutely thrilled ... '

SECTION C: REPORTING

C1 *The list.* Get students to suggest ways in which either Clare or Maisy might use the listed expressions to tell the story of what happened.
Suggested answers

1 Clare: 'I was quite taken aback for a moment. I thought they were going to ask us to go with them.' (= startled, not sure what to say)

Maisy: 'When I mentioned Nice, she seemed quite taken aback.'

2 Both: 'I was/She was obviously wondering how I/she could get out of it.' (= escape from, avoid going to Nice)

3 Clare: 'It would have been awkward if she had invited us.' (= difficult, embarrassing)

4 Both: 'I/She was rather embarrassed, having already said that I/she had made plans for the summer.'

5 Maisy: 'When I offered her the house, she accepted immediately.'

6 Clare: 'It was quite a relief when it turned out she wasn't inviting us after all.'
'You can imagine my relief when ... '

C2 *Reporting.* Students now write reports, either individually, in pairs or groups, or for homework. This time the reports are addressed to someone specific — Maisy's husband or Clare's hus-

Unit 6 Part one

band. Approximately half the reports should be from Clare's point of view, and half from Maisy's point of view.

Two possible reports

Clare: '... Well, then suddenly she asked me if we had any plans for the summer. I was quite taken aback for a moment, and I was terribly afraid she was going to suggest that we all go on holiday together — you know they usually go to Nice. It would have been very awkward to refuse, and I was quite relieved when it turned out that she was offering us their house in Cornwall while they were away. Well, I was thrilled, and accepted the offer immediately. It was rather embarrassing, actually, because I'd already started saying that we'd already made plans for the summer, but I don't think she noticed. So we've got their house for the summer. Of course, she only offered it because she's hoping you'll do the gardening for her, but all the same ...'

Maisy: 'Well, I've found someone to look after the garden. Clare and Tony are having the house while we're away. Actually, it was rather strange — we were having coffee this morning and I casually asked her about her plans for the summer. She was obviously rather taken aback, and hesitated a bit — I think she was wondering why I wanted to know. And when I said that we were going to Nice, she immediately told me that they had already made arrangements for the summer. She was looking a bit embarrassed by this time — she must have thought I was going to invite them to come with us! However, as soon as I told her that I was offering her the house, not our company, she accepted immediately. She was absolutely delighted — and obviously relieved that she didn't have to make up any more excuses ...'

Unit 6 Part two

Part two: Expressing the feeling

SECTION A: RECOGNITION

A1 Feeling fine

Follow the same general procedure as for unit 1, A1 'Who wants what?' (see notes, p. 25).

Suggested answers
1 Politician, sportsman, etc., making a speech to his supporters after winning an election, sports contest, etc.
2 A wine connoisseur identifying and savouring a very good wine.
3 Someone who has predicted that the weather would become cold, and is delighted at proving her friend wrong.
4 Someone in a pub, bar, etc., finishing his first drink and ordering another.
5 Someone who has just mended something, removed a stain, repainted something, etc., looking at what she's done with satisfaction.
6 Two friends recalling a very funny episode in a film, play, TV programme or book. ('I nearly died' = 'I nearly died of laughter')
7 An enthusiastic member of an audience at a performance (e.g. a concert) calling for more.
8 Two people constructing a quiz or problem-solving activity (e.g. a recognition exercise), delighted because they've thought up a difficult question.

A2 Hello...goodbye

This exercise presents formulae used in opening remarks when meeting people, and in closing remarks when 'leave-taking'. In each case, the person is expressing delight, pleasure or gratitude of some kind. Point out to the class that both remarks are made by the same person in each case, and they should imagine a considerable period of time between the two remarks.
Follow the same general procedure as for A1-type recognition exercises.

Answers
1 Two old friends or acquaintances meet by chance. They have a friendly chat.

Unit 6 Part two

2 Someone is introduced to a person he wanted to meet (e.g. someone famous, or someone who could give him advice or information).
3 A has asked B to come, and B is doing A a favour by coming. B might be a doctor, plumber, car mechanic, etc.
4 Host to guest at e.g. a dinner party.
5 A wants to arrange an appointment with B, and happens to see him. They make their appointment.
6 Compère at a variety show, etc., introducing a guest to the audience, and thanking him after his appearance.
7 A agrees to help B in some way. Afterwards, she replies to B's thanks.

SECTION B: PRACTICE

> *Basic structures*
> past conditional (B1, B2)
> *could/might* + *have done* (B2)

B1 What a relief

Language functions: Expressing relief because you have finished or achieved something; expressing relief because of a 'narrow escape'.

This exercise contrasts the two language functions above. The expressions are of three kinds:
1 for expressing satisfaction with an achievement
  (suitable for picture A only)
2 for expressing relief because of a 'narrow escape'
  (suitable for picture B only)
3 for expressing either of the two functions
  (suitable for both pictures)

Structural difficulties: None.

Stage 1 Answers: picture A: a,b,c,d   picture B: b,c,e,f,g
Stage 2 Procedure: Follow the same general procedure as for unit 1, B1 'Wishful thinking' (see notes, p. 28). In general, picture A captions will be suitable for the first of each pair of pictures, and picture B captions for the second.

72

Unit 6 Part two

B2 A narrow escape

Language functions: Two or more people together expressing relief because of a narrow escape; speculating about what might have happened, but didn't.

There are three kinds of expressions practised in this exercise:
1 Formulae for expressing relief ('It's a good thing . . . ', 'It's lucky . . . ', 'Thank goodness'). These were introduced in B1, above.
2 Expressions used simply to mention that things might have been different (bubbles on left of picture).
3 Expressions used for speculating about *what* might have happened (bubbles on right of picture).

Structural difficulties:
1 The past conditional, which is central to this exercise. Students speculate about what *would/could/might have happened*. So it is essential that students are familiar with past conditional structures before they do the exercise.
2 Use of *otherwise* (meaning 'if that hadn't happened').
    Cf. i) 'It's lucky the pilot had a parachute. *If he hadn't had had one*, he would have been killed.'
       ii) 'It's lucky the pilot had a parachute. *Otherwise* he would have been killed.'

Procedure

Stage 1 Discuss the picture and the situation. Ask students to complete the onlookers' remarks.
Example answers
'It's a good thing it missed the supermarket.'
'It's lucky the pilot managed to bail out in time.'
'Thank goodness it landed in the field.'
'I hate to think what would've happened (if it had landed in the road).'
'Who knows how many people would have been killed (if . . .).'
'Imagine what might've happened if it had been a Boeing 747.'
'Yes, if it had (hit the supermarket) it would have flattened it.'
'Yes, it could easily have come down in the middle of the road.'
'Yes, otherwise he wouldn't have stood a chance.'
'And then it would have killed hundreds of people.'

Unit 6 Part two

Stage 2 Divide the class into groups.
Each group could improvise a conversation about the aeroplane before going on to the other situations, so that they get an idea of how the conversations should develop.
Each of the conversations should be left fairly free, and students should make comments in any order they like.
Stage 3 As a round-up, ask each group what ideas they had for their situations.

B3 The perfect present

Language functions: Showing that you are delighted with something you are given; expressing gratitude.

Structural difficulties: None.

This exercise presents and practises typical formulae used when giving and receiving presents.

Procedure
Stage 1 Ask students to suggest other ways of *offering* a present, e.g. 'Here's a . . . for you'; 'I thought you might like a . . . '; 'I decided to get you a . . . '.
Stage 2 Go through the two lists of replies. Discuss the important factors in choosing which expressions to use for each item, e.g. value; usefulness; beauty; how much the person wanted/expected it.
Stage 3 *Groupwork.* This can be done in two ways:
  Either students sit in groups and give 'presents' to each other
  or students move freely around the class giving 'presents' to whoever they like.
Instead of writing names of things on pieces of paper, students can be given pictures of objects (cut out of a magazine) which they can use as presents.

SECTION C: FREE EXPRESSION

C1 Summer course

Language functions: Expressing satisfaction with your situation; expressing dissatisfaction with your situation.

Unit 6 Part two

This is a *half-and-half improvisation*. Follow the same general procedure as for unit 2, C1 'Old and new' (see notes, p. 40).

C2 Having a lovely time...

Language function: Expressing your enjoyment and appreciation of a place in writing.

This is a *guessing game*. Follow the same general procedure as for unit 1, C2 'Just the job' (see notes, p. 32).

In this exercise there are two elements to guess: the place and the person. Each group chooses one of the twenty-five combinations, and writes a postcard from which it should be possible to guess both elements. No example is given in the students' book. One is given below, which can be read to the class as an introduction if you think it necessary:

'... I'm having a wonderful time here — sitting in the sun all day long taking in the fresh air and the beautiful views, and spending the evenings in the most delightful cafes. Yesterday I even went on a chair-lift — I was a bit worried at first and thought I'd freeze to death, but a very nice young man helped me get on it and wrapped me up in a large blanket — I really enjoyed it.'
Answer: Old lady in the Alps.

Unit 7 Indignation/Annoyance

Part one: Talking about the feeling

SECTION A: DISCUSSION

A1 Listening and **A2 Facts**

Procedure (For more detail on procedure see notes on unit 1, p. 19.)
Stage 1 Books closed. Play the dialogue once.
Stage 2 Elicit information, playing the tape again where necessary.
Stage 3 Books open. Students follow as tape is played again.
Stage 4 Facts questions are answered briefly to summarise the preceding discussion.

Answers
1 They're strangers. Daniel is a barman, Clive is a customer.
2 In a pub, or the bar of a hotel.
3 He wants some more beer (half a pint).
4 He refuses to serve Clive. It's closing time, and he'd be breaking the law if he served him.
5 They are drinking and ordering drinks.
6 The closing time rule does not apply to overnight guests of the pub/hotel.
7 He thinks the other people are not residents at all, but friends of the landlord, and that he is being discriminated against.
8 He leaves the bar, swearing.

A3 Language

Procedure (For more detail on procedure see notes on unit 1, p. 21.)
Stage 1 Students answer the questions individually or in pairs.
Stage 2 Go through the answers with the whole class.

Answers
1 a,d,e   d = generally unpleasant.
           a,e = quick to take offence or lose one's temper.

Unit 7 Part one

                c: Clive *gets* angry, but *angry* is not generally used to describe *types* of people.
                b: if Clive were moody, we would expect him to get depressed, not indignant.
2 a,b,e   e = angry at being treated unjustly.
                c: you do not *get* displeased. Also, *displeased* is rather old-fashioned, and implies authority, e.g. 'You have been rude. Your father is displeased.'
                d: *excited* is in general a positive feeling (see unit 2, part one).
3 a,d   *angry* is not an absolute adjective; *furious* is.
4 a,b,c   d would imply that he was Daniel's boss (see note to no. 2, above).
                e would imply that he was worried about it.
5 a,b   c would imply that he wanted to cry.
6 b   *to accuse someone of* = you're saying he did something bad.
                to blame someone for = something bad has happened and you're saying it is his fault.
7 b,c   b is much more common than c. Usually you swear at people and curse things, e.g. 'He cursed his bad luck.'

SECTION B: PRACTICE

B1 Bad feeling

    Stage 1   Go through the introduction and examples with the class. Point out that *indignant* is used especially meaning angry because (a) you are being treated unfairly (e.g. Clive in the dialogue) or (b) somebody else is being treated unfairly (e.g. Josie in the exercise).
    Stage 2   Discuss which of them could be *angry* or *furious*:
                Janet could be angry.
                Jasmine could be angry and furious.
                Josie could be angry and furious.
                Note: June, Janet and Jasmine are also *disappointed* and *upset*.
    Stage 3   In groups or pairs, students choose appropriate expressions to describe the feelings of the seven people in the exercise.
                Suggested answers
                a) annoyed   b) indignant   c) offended (hurt,

Unit 7 Part one

     annoyed)   d) hurt   e) indignant   f) annoyed (indignant)   g) offended
  Stage 4 Relating the language to the dialogue:
     Clive: 'I was indignant about the way I was being treated.'
     Daniel: 'He seemed offended/annoyed when I refused to serve him.'
     Clive: 'By the end I was very angry/absolutely furious.'

B2 Story line

In this exercise, students have to construct the example themselves, using the picture and the listed expressions.
Suggested answer
Car driver: 'His lorry was blocking my drive, so I asked him to move it. He refused to do anything about it, and made some feeble excuse about delivering something next door. That really annoyed me, so I told him exactly what I thought of him. It didn't make any difference, though.'
Lorry driver: 'I was delivering some furniture the other day when the man next door came up and asked me to move my lorry so he could get his car out. I tried to explain that I couldn't move it straight away, but he wouldn't listen. He suddenly lost his temper and started swearing at me, so I decided to make him wait.'

Procedure
Stage 1 Together, the class construct reports for the car driver and lorry driver.
Stage 2 In groups or pairs, they construct further reports for the other three pictures.
Stage 3 Go through the answers with the whole class.
Stage 4 Relating the language to the dialogue: see the two reports in section C, below.

SECTION C: REPORTING

C1 *The list.* Get students to suggest ways in which either Clive or Daniel might use the listed expressions to tell the story of what happened.

Unit 7 Part one

Suggested answers
1. Clive: 'I pointed out that some other people were still being served.'
   Daniel: 'I pointed out to him that it was closing time.'
2. Clive: 'He made some excuse about it being closing time.'
   Daniel: See 1, above.
3. Daniel: 'He insisted on being served.'
4. Clive: 'I found his manner very offhand.'
5. Both: 'He was very argumentative.'
6. Daniel: 'When I refused to serve him, he took offence immediately.'
7. Daniel: 'In the end, he stormed out, swearing.'

C2 *Reporting.* Students now write reports, either individually, in pairs or groups, or for homework. Approximately half the reports should be from Clive's point of view and half from Daniel's point of view.

Two possible reports
Clive: '... Well, I thought I'd have a last beer before I went home. But when I went up to the bar to ask for one, the barman refused to serve me — said it was closing time. There were several other people there, and he was serving them all right; and when I pointed that out to him, he made some excuse about them being residents. I was already quite annoyed, but that made me absolutely furious; quite apart from the fact that he was obviously trying to make a fool out of me, he had a very offhand manner which I found most offensive. There wasn't much I could do about it, of course, but at least I made sure he knew what I thought of him before I left ...'

Daniel: '... It was round about closing time on Saturday. I'd just called time, when some drunk came up and demanded half of bitter. I told him as nicely as I could that he was too late. He seemed to take offence at that, and wanted to know why the other people there were still being served. They were guests of the hotel, of course, but when I tried to explain that to him, he got most indignant. In fact, he completely lost his temper and started accusing me of giving him unfair treatment. It didn't last long, though — he soon saw he wasn't going to get anywhere, and he stormed out of the bar, swearing and shouting like a madman. You should have seen him!'

Unit 7 Part two

Part two: Expressing the feeling

SECTION A: RECOGNITION

A1 All steamed up

Follow the same general procedure as for unit 1, A1 'Who wants what?' (see notes, p. 25).

Suggested answers
1 A landowner or game-keeper has caught someone who claims to be bird-watching. He doesn't believe him, because of something he is carrying, e.g. a gun.
2 A complaint about someone who has plenty of money but is very mean with it, or who keeps borrowing from other people.
3 Someone who expects someone else to have tidied a room (e.g. parent to child), but doesn't think it has been done properly.
4 A desperate warning by someone who is being cheated, robbed, blackmailed, etc., meaning that the other person will get caught.
5 A slogan, probably written, protesting against the dangers of large lorries. Might be seen at a protest meeting about motorways, road-widening, etc.
6 Someone who wants to discuss something serious is complaining that the other person refuses to take him seriously.
7 Parent, teacher, etc. attempting to stop child/children talking, playing, etc.
8 Someone who is annoyed that her advice has been rejected, meaning 'If you refuse to take my advice, it's your own responsibility.'
9 Reply to e.g. 'I wonder where my book is', 'I'll take my book now', etc., meaning 'It isn't *your* book, it's *mine*.'

A2 Going to extremes

This is a *matching exercise*. Follow the same general procedure as for unit 1, A2 'Best wishes' (see notes, p. 27).

This exercise presents formulae used for expressing strong indignation. The differences between them depend not on strength of feeling but on *what* you are reacting to. The four general categories are:
a) someone *saying* something offensive

Unit 7 Part two

b) someone *doing* something he has no right to do
c) someone ignoring your advice
d) someone *repeatedly* doing something you don't like

Answers
a) 2 How dare you!
    4 I *beg* your pardon!
    7 What do you mean?
b) 6 What do you think you're doing?
    2 How dare you! (possibly)
c) 3 Have it your own way!
    9 All right, if that's the way you feel about it!
d) 1 That does it!
    5 Now look what you've done!
    8 That's all I need!

SECTION B: PRACTICE

> *Basic structures*
> past conditional structures (B1)
> *should(n't)* + *have done* (B1)
> *ought to* + *do/have done* (B2)
> *could/might* + *have done* (B3)
> indirect speech + *would/were going to* (B3)

B1 Finding fault

Language functions: Accusing, blaming and criticising in informal situations.

Structural difficulties: Difference between:
1 'It's your fault (*that*) ... (we're late; I had to change; I spilt the wine)'
= something has happened, and you're saying it's the other person's fault.
2 'It's your fault *for* ... (spilling the wine on my dress; taking so long to change; leaving your handbag on the floor)'
= you're saying *why* it's the other person's fault.

Procedure: Follow the same general procedure as for unit 1, B1 'Wishful thinking' (see notes, p. 28). Here again, the first set of pictures tell a story, which should be gone through in detail before doing the exercise.

Possible answers
'It's all your fault we're late.'
'It's all your fault for spilling the wine over my dress.'
'You shouldn't have taken so long changing your dress.'
'If you hadn't left your handbag on the floor, I wouldn't have tripped up and spilled the wine.'
'It was you that spilled the wine, not me.' etc.

Some ways of denying accusations:
'Nonsense', 'Rubbish', etc.
'It isn't my fault at all.'
'That wasn't my fault.'
'But how was I to know . . . ?'
'What do you mean?'
'Not at all.'
'I couldn't help it.'

B2 What a nerve!

Language functions: 'Shared' indignation, i.e. two or more people expressing indignation about something that affects them.

Structural difficulties: Use of *the way* as a sentence connective (see notes for unit 4, B2 'How do you do it?', p. 56).

Procedure
Stage 1   Read through the newspaper article and discuss what specific things the people of Whimsy might be indignant about, and why.
Stage 2   Ask students to complete the remarks of the people in the pub.
These are of two kinds:
a) *about things that are happening/have happened:*
'They've got no right to take decisions like that without consulting us.'
'What do they mean by building an airport so close to Whimsy?'
'They can't just build airports wherever they feel like it.'
'I think it's shocking/disgusting/disgraceful/appalling the way they kept it a secret for so long.'
b) *about things that aren't happening/haven't happened:*
'Why couldn't they have built it somewhere else?'
'They might have found out what the public thought first.'

Unit 7 Part two

'The thing that really annoys me is the way they didn't tell us about it till yesterday.'

Stage 3 In the groupwork practice, students should talk about something they *really* feel indignant about. For this reason, the choice of topic has been left open; this should be done before you continue with the exercise. Choose either one general topic or a number of connected topics.

Stage 4 Give a short preparation stage in which students think about the topic and make notes. They should *not* write exactly what they will say, as this will destroy the spontaneity of the exercise.

Stage 5 Form the class into groups of at least four to discuss the topic.

Stage 6 You can round the exercise up by asking groups to report briefly on what they said.

B3 Broken promises

Language functions: Getting annoyed with someone who has let you down; making excuses to justify yourself.

Structural difficulties: None.

Procedure
This is a *skeleton conversation.* Follow the same general procedure as for unit 2, B3 'Have you heard?' (see notes, p. 39).
A possible version of the conversation:
Dave: What happened to the shopping you said you were going to do?
Paul: Shopping? Oh, well I didn't have time.
Dave: Hmm. Surely you could have got in a few tins, or something.
Paul: Look, I'm sorry, but I was just too busy.
Dave: Huh! Just like you to promise to do something and then then not do it!

Note: In each of the situations, Paul's second excuse can be either a repetition of the first (as in the example above), or a different excuse (e.g. 'The shop was closed').

Unit 7 Part two

SECTION C: FREE EXPRESSION

C1 Dangerous drivers

Language functions: Accusing, blaming and criticising; expressing indignation about what someone has done.

This exercise gives further practice of the language introduced in B1.

This is a *half-and-half improvisation.* Follow the same general procedure as for unit 2, C1 'Old and new' (see notes, p. 40). As the conversation will vary greatly according to the personality of the speakers, this is a particularly good time to do the interaction stage *twice* (as suggested in unit 2), with different As and Bs confronting each other the second time.

C2 More Manwick developments

Language function: 'Shared' indignation about something that affects you.

This exercise gives further practice of the language introduced in B2.

This is a *group interview.* There is also an exercise like this in part two, section C of units 8, 9 and 12.

Procedure: This exercise has two distinct stages: a *preparation stage* and an *interaction stage.*
Stage 1   Preparation
  Divide the class into five groups; assign *one* of the five roles to each group. Working together, each group prepares what their character might say, making brief notes if they like. It is important that they should *all* be equally prepared, as they will all have to perform their role.
Stage 2   Interaction
  Students form into new groups. Each new group contains all five characters. The journalist in each group interviews the other four, and 'chairs' any discussion that may develop.
  Obviously, this exercise is simplest to organise for classes of ten, fifteen, twenty, twenty-five, etc. However it is very easy to adapt it for classes of any number of students by

Unit 7 Part two

i) cutting out one of the roles so that there are only four people taking part in the interview.
ii) 'doubling up', so that in one group there are, say, Mr and Mrs Phipps instead of just Mr Phipps.

Unit 8 Surprise

Part one: Talking about the feeling

SECTION A: LISTENING AND DISCUSSION

A1 Listening and **A2** Facts

Procedure (For more detail on procedure see notes on unit 1, p. 19.)
Stage 1 Books closed. Play the dialogue once.
Stage 2 Elicit information, playing the tape again where necessary.
Stage 3 Books open. Students follow as tape is played again.
Stage 4 Facts questions are answered briefly to summarise the preceding discussion.

Answers
1 Old friends (from school, university, same street, etc.).
2 Abroad, probably in a developing country. Either in an official building (e.g. UNESCO offices) or a public place (e.g. hotel foyer).
3 Archie has been there a long time — months or years. David has just arrived.
4 Engineer, agronomist, etc. He is about to take up an advisory/administrative post concerned with irrigation.
5 '... going back to England'; '... retiring'; 'been given the sack'; '... been here for years' etc.
6 He's just realised something, and he's giving himself time to think.
7 Archie is MacDonald. He's the man David is taking over from.

A3 Language

Procedure (For more detail on procedure see notes on unit 1, p. 21.)
Stage 1 Students answer the questions individually or in pairs.
Stage 2 Go through the answers with the whole class.

Unit 8 Part one

Answers
1 a,d   b would mean he was *looking for* Archie.
         c is not used metaphorically in this context.
2 a,c,d   c and d are stronger than a.
         b = *unpleasantly* surprised.
         See B1 'Surprising news', below.
3 b,d,e   a and c: *all* coincidences are unusual/unlikely.
         b, d and e are used as intensifiers.
4 b   a: you can only realise *facts* (see no. 6, below).
         c: he does remember him — otherwise he couldn't recognise him.
5 c   a: if they were changing places, Archie would also be replacing David.
6 a   b: for *recognise*, see no. 4, above.
         c: *learns* = he is told by someone else.
         d: 'thinks' would mean that he is mistaken.

SECTION B: PRACTICE

B1 Surprising news

Procedure
Stage 1   Go through the example with the class.
Stage 2   Discuss the difference between the four adjectives.
         You're *surprised* if something happens that you don't expect.
         astonished/amazed = *very surprised.*
         shocked = *unpleasantly surprised.*
Stage 3   In groups or pairs, students talk about their feelings in the seven situations given, using *two sentences* for each answer (one beginning 'I was (surprised) . . . ', the other 'It came as . . . ').
Stage 4   Go through the answers with the whole class.
         Answers
         a) shocked   b) amazed/astonished   c) amazed/astonished   d) amazed/astonished   e) shocked
         f) surprised   g) surprised
         (b, c and d could be *surprised*, and f and g *astonished/amazed*, depending on the strength of your reaction.)
Stage 5   Relating the language to the dialogue:
         Both: 'I was surprised/astonished/amazed to see Archie/David.'

Unit 8 Part one

>David: 'It came as a great surprise to discover that I was taking over from Archie.'

B2   Story line

Procedure
Stage 1   Go through the example headline and paragraph with the class.
Stage 2   In groups or pairs, students make similar reports for the four headlines given. Since this is a fairly straightforward and short exercise, groups that finish quickly may make up their own headline and story.
Stage 3   Go through the answers with the whole class.
Stage 4   Relating the language to the dialogue:
>David: 'It was my first visit to the office. I walked in and was astonished to see that Archie was there, sitting at a desk. I could hardly believe my eyes when I saw him — I mean, he was the last person I'd expected to see.'

SECTION C: REPORTING

C1   *The list.* Get students to suggest ways in which David might use the listed expressions to tell the story of what happened.

Suggested answers
1 What an extraordinary coincidence, meeting Archie like that.
2 I had no idea that Archie was in Bangladesh/was the person I was replacing.
3 I happened to be in the Embassy when . . .
I happened to see Archie sitting at a desk.
(= I was there by chance.)
4 It suddenly dawned on me that Archie and MacDonald were the same person.
(= I suddenly realised.)
5 I hadn't connected the name of MacDonald with Archie.

C2   *Reporting.* Students now write reports, either individually, in pairs or groups, or for homework. This time all the reports are from David's point of view, and form part of a letter home to his wife.

Possible report
' . . . An extraordinary thing happened just after I got here. I

Unit 8 Part two

was in the bar at the Embassy, having a quiet drink, when I suddenly noticed an old school-friend of mine, Archie — I've told you about him hundreds of times. Anyway, there he was sitting next to me at the bar. I didn't even recognise him at first — after all, he was the very last person I'd expected to meet in Bangladesh! We got talking, and I started telling him about the UNESCO job ... and then it suddenly dawned on me that he must be the very person I was taking over from. What an amazing coincidence! I'd known all the time that I was replacing a man called MacDonald, but I hadn't connected the name with Archie at all ... '

Part two: Expressing the feeling

SECTION A: RECOGNITION

A1 Surprise surprise

Follow the same general procedure as for unit 1, A1 'Who wants what?' (see notes, p. 25). As in unit 1, all the remarks in this exercise are replies to what someone else has said.

Suggested answers
1 Two people fishing (or catching insects, butterflies, etc.). Reply to e.g. 'I haven't caught a single fish.'
2 Two people studying/doing homework together, e.g. reading a comprehension passage, poem, etc. Reply to e.g. 'There we are — I've finished.'
3 Talking about a baby, child or pet that has just been fed. Reply to e.g. 'He seems to be hungry.'
4 The other person is talking about something he did (at length).
5 Someone with a regional or foreign accent has been given a speech prize, job, etc. Reply to e.g. 'They've given Peter that job in the BBC.'
6 An important person in the village is being treated badly in some way, e.g. he's been removed from his job in the Council. Reply to e.g. 'I see Major Hibley's been given the sack.'
7 Two people see a house (on fire, with suspicious light on inside, or in a newspaper picture, etc.) and realise that it is theirs. Reply to e.g. 'Hey, isn't that our house with the fire engine outside?'

Unit 8 Part two

8 Someone who is being told that she has a visitor or a phone call. Reply to e.g. 'It's for you.'
9 Two people playing a board game, e.g. chess or draughts. One person thinks the other has made a stupid move, then realises how clever it is. Reply to e.g. 'Your move' or could be a response to the person making the move in silence.

A2 In a manner of speaking

This is a *matching exercise*, but it is different from most others in the book because it is concerned with *intonation*.

The exercise introduces the use of tag questions for expressing surprise (these are practised in part two section B of the unit). It also gives insight into how the same remark can express different feelings according to how it is said.

Procedure
Stage 1 Play the tape to the whole class (at least twice). Students note down what they think the answers are.
Stage 2 Discuss the answers together, and ask students to suggest what *other* feelings are expressed in each case.
   Answers: 1 d   2 e   3 c   4 a   5 b
   Other feelings: 1 —   2 Sympathy
   3–4 Shock, indignation   5 Admiration

SECTION B: PRACTICE

> *Basic structures*
> indirect speech (B1)
> tag questions (B2, B3)
> short forms (B2)
> indirect questions (B3)

B1 False impressions

Language functions: Expressing surprise when something you expected *doesn't* happen; expressing surprise when something you didn't expect *does* happen.
This exercise contrasts expressions used for these two language functions.

Unit 8 Part two

Structural difficulties
1 Expressions a, b, c, d and e are all 'reported thought' structures, and follow the same sequence of tenses rule as indirect speech, i.e. because the sentence begins in the past, it must continue in the past.
    e.g. 'I *thought* I *heard* a knock.'
    'I *didn't think* it *rained* here.'
2 *Expect*, in the sense used here, is followed by (pro)noun + to + infinitive
    e.g. 'I never expected it to rain here.'
    'I never expected Chelsea to win.'

Procedure: Follow the same general procedure as for unit 1 B1 'Wishful thinking' (see notes, p. 28).

Stage 1   Other formulae for expressing surprise
          How incredible/amazing/astonishing!
          I can't/don't believe it!
          That's funny/odd/strange!
          Good Heavens/Lord! etc.

Stage 2   Captions for picture 1
          c) e.g. I was sure someone was at the door.
          d) e.g. I could've sworn I heard a knock.
          e) e.g. I was quite certain someone was there.
          Captions for picture 2
          a) e.g. Who would've thought it would rain in Egypt?
          b) e.g. I didn't know it rained in the desert.
          f) I never expected it to rain here.

B2   Tall stories

Language functions: Announcing surprising news, reacting with strong surprise to something someone tells you.

Structural difficulties: This exercise practises formulae for announcing and reacting to surprising news. The expressions for *reacting* with surprise are of four types:
1 A 'short form' repetition of what the other person said:
    e.g. 'You haven't!' 'You didn't!' 'She isn't!'
2 A 'short form' repetition plus a tag question:
    e.g. 'You haven't, have you?' 'You didn't, did you?' 'She isn't, is she?'
3 A 'short question':
    e.g. 'Have you really?' 'Did you really?' 'Is she really?'
4 *can't* + infinitive:
    e.g. 'You can't have done!' 'She can't be!'

Unit 8 Part two

The second part of the exercise practises these forms using different tenses, persons and auxiliaries. It is important that students have a good general grasp of tags and short forms before doing the exercise.

Procedure
Stage 1 After going through the example and the main structures, ask students to suggest replies to each of the five remarks.
Stage 2 Divide the class into pairs. Each pair improvises four-line conversations beginning with the remarks given.
e.g. A: Did you know? The Beatles are together again.
     B: They aren't, are they?
     A: Yes, and what's more, they're making a new LP.
     B: They can't be!
Stage 3 Students form into groups of four. They improvise similar four-line conversations, inventing their own pieces of surprising news.

B3 Out of the blue

Language function: Two people both expressing surprise at news they hear about someone else.

Structural difficulties
1 The expression 'Whatever made him (+ infinitive without *to*) ... ?' This means the same as 'Why did he ... ?' but expresses surprise more strongly.
2 The rather unusual use of *should* in 'It seems strange that he should ... ' *Should* is used in this way in other expressions of surprise or puzzlement:
e.g. 'I can't understand why he should ... '
     'I'm surprised that he should ... '

Procedure: This is a *skeleton conversation*. Follow the same general procedure as for unit 2, B3 'Have you heard?' (see notes, p. 39).

A possible version of the conversation:
Pam: I've just had a letter from Richard. Apparently he's started going to keep-fit classes.
Sid: Good Lord! That's incredible! Whatever made him decide to do a thing like that?
Pam: Well, he is rather fat, you know.
Sid: Yes, but all the same. It's not like him to do anything so energetic.
Pam: Yes, it does seem a bit odd, doesn't it?

Unit 8 Part two

SECTION C: FREE EXPRESSION

C1 Jude the Obscure

Language function: Showing you are surprised and puzzled when you find out something about someone else.

This exercise gives further practice of the language introduced in B1 and B2.

Procedure: This exercise works in a similar way to 'More Manwick developments', unit 7, C2 (see notes, p. 84), except that the final stage is an informal discussion instead of a formal interview.

Stage 1 Preparation
Divide the class into four groups; assign *one* of the four roles (A, B, C, D) to each group. Working together each group studies the instructions for their role *only*, and works out a consistent story about Jude, adding details of their own.

Stage 2 Interaction
Students form into new groups, each group containing all four roles. They improvise a discussion about Jude. Although this should be a free exercise, remind students that they can use the expressions of surprise they have practised where appropriate.

C2 Newsdesk

Language function: Expressing astonishment on hearing news.

This exercise gives further practice of the language introduced in B2.

This is a *guessing game*. Follow the same general procedure as for unit 1, C2 'Just the job' (see notes, p. 32).

The situation in the example: The man has seen a flying saucer land. It flew over his house, and landed nearby. Some strange looking 'men' got out. They then made him a cup of tea, or asked the man for a cup of tea.

Unit 9 Disappointment/Regret

Part one: Talking about the feeling

SECTION A: LISTENING AND DISCUSSION

A1 Listening and **A2 Facts**

Procedure (For more detail on procedure see notes on unit 1, p. 19.)
Stage 1 Books closed. Play dialogue once.
Stage 2 Elicit information, playing the tape again where necessary.
Stage 3 Books open. Students follow as tape is played again.
Stage 4 'Facts' questions are answered briefly to summarise the preceding discussion.

Answers
1 Old friends. They have known each other for a long time.
2 Housewife.
3 Doing the housework, shopping, etc.
4 When she was a university student (she didn't take her degree).
5 He doesn't help her in the house. He doesn't realise how hard she works. He doesn't notice her very much.
6 She told her not to get married, and predicted the very situation that Susan is now in.

A3 Language

Procedure (For more detail on procedure see notes on unit 1, p. 21.)
Stage 1 Students answer the questions individually or in pairs.
Srage 2 Go through the answers with the whole class.

Answers
1 a,b,f   c is also correct in North-of-England English.
          b, c and f are informal.
2 b,c   *disappointed* is usually used about particular things or events, e.g. 'She was disappointed with the party/her wedding presents'. See B1 'Feeling low', below.

94

Unit 9 Part one

3 c   a and b: they probably *do* like and want her. The problem is that they 'take her for granted', i.e. they don't seem to notice how much she is doing.
4 a,c,e   *regret* is followed by . . . *ing* or *that* . . . , not by the infinitive.
5 d   *wish* + *past perfect*: she is regretting the past.
6 c   *wish* + *past tense*: she is dissatisfied with her present situation, i.e. she hasn't got a job.

SECTION B: PRACTICE

B1   Feeling low

Procedure
Stage 1   Go through the examples with the class.
Stage 2   Discuss the differences in meaning between the different expressions by talking about the different aspects of Jack's life as a sailor.

dissatisfied:	he thought that his pay and working conditions weren't good enough.
disappointed:	he had expected the places he visited to be nice (beautiful, exciting, etc.) but they weren't.
tired of/sick of/fed up with:	he had spent so much time cleaning the decks that he had had enough of it, and wanted a change.
disillusioned:	he had believed that life as a sailor would be wonderful, but his dreams were destroyed by actually being a sailor and finding out what it was really like.

Stage 3   In groups or pairs, students use the listed expressions to talk about the feelings of the people in the exercise.
Suggested answers
a) tired of/sick of/fed up with   b) disappointed
c) disillusioned   d) dissatisfied   e) tired of/fed up with/sick of   f) disappointed   g) disillusioned

Stage 4   Relating the language to the dialogue:
Cathy: 'Susan is dissatisfied with the way things are going/her husband, etc.'
'She is disillusioned with life in general/being a housewife/married life.'

Unit 9 Part one

> Both: 'She is/I am tired of (sick of/fed up with) sitting at home all day, etc.'

B2 Upsetting events

Procedure

Stage 1 Go through the examples with the class. Point out that *upset* has a very general meaning (see also unit 7, B1 'Bad feeling', notes, p. 77). This exercise concentrates on two aspects of being upset, namely *disappointment* and *shock*.

Stage 2 Students talk about Peter in the five situations given.
Suggested answers
1 disappointment   2 shock   3 disappointment
4 shock   5 shock

Stage 3 As an extension, you could ask students to talk about things that happened to them that came as a disappointment or shock to them.

SECTION C: REPORTING

This report is different from those in the other units in that it is part of a short story in a magazine *about* Susan, rather than told by Susan herself.

C1 *The list.* Get students to suggest how they might use the listed expressions in a story about Susan.

Suggested answers
1 Susan sighed/gave a sigh as she finished the washing up ...
2 If she hadn't married Paul, she could have made a career for herself.
   Her marriage had prevented her from taking up a career.
3 Five years of married life had left her feeling bored and frustrated.
   She was so frustrated; there were so many things she wanted to do.
4 She couldn't stand the dull, boring routine.
   Her whole time seemed to be taken up with dull, routine work.
5 Everything seemed so pointless.
6 She and her husband had begun to drift apart.

C2 *Reporting.* Students now write reports, either individually, in pairs or groups, or for homework. Here are two possible beginnings to the story. The first is fairly close to the dialogue; the second is much freer:

a) 'With a sigh, Susan sank into the deep armchair. When she had got married at the age of 19, she had been happy to give up her career for the man she loved. Now, after five years of married life, she was completely disillusioned, and regretted what she had done. Her mind went back over those five years — years of babies, housework and exhausted evenings in front of the television. How useless and frustrated she felt. She wouldn't have minded so much, if her husband appreciated her more. But he and the children took her completely for granted. She wished she had a job or a hobby, but the dull routine of being a housewife seemed to exclude everything else . . . '

b) 'Susan sighed as she picked up the two halves of the plate from the kitchen floor. Just a little accident, but to her it symbolised the breaking point of her marriage. She couldn't hide it any more. She was fed up, completely fed up with being a housewife. Yet, just three years before, the thought of being Peter's wife had been all she had wanted in the world. Well, she had got it. She had married at 19, had left Durham the year before she would have got her degree, and had had a son and then a daughter. And somehow, as she had become busier with the housework and the children, Peter had drifted away from her. He hardly noticed her when he came home — if he came home at all; the intimate conversation which had filled their lives had been replaced by the TV. Susan knew that her life was becoming more pointless every day. She decided to tell someone, someone she could trust, someone who could give her some good advice . . . The doorbell rang . . . '

Part two: Expressing the feeling

SECTION A: RECOGNITION

A1 What's wrong?

Follow the same general procedure as for unit 1, A1 'Who wants what?' (see notes, p. 25).

Unit 9 Part two

Suggested answers
1 Two people have been to a party (film, play, etc.) where either there was no music or the music wasn't very good. Otherwise, they have enjoyed themselves.
2 Someone who has just tried a product for the first time, probably a breakfast cereal or a detergent, and didn't like it. It was either recommended to them, or they had seen it advertised.
3 Hosts who are disappointed that their guests didn't appreciate a special dish they had prepared.
4 Someone who has moved from a house with a garden to a house or flat without a garden.
5 Someone who has tried several times to make a phone call, fails to get through again, and gives up trying.
6 Someone who is short of money has just received a bill, or heard that he has to pay some money unexpectedly.
7 Someone has been reminded about a dental appointment. She is either too late or almost too late, or she doesn't want to go.
8 Someone who is watching TV when the commercials come on, or reading a magazine with a lot of advertisements in it.

A2 Life at the top

This is a *matching exercise*. Follow the same general procedure as for unit 1, A2 'Best wishes' (see notes, p. 27).

This exercise presents formulae for expressing regret. The differences between the expressions depend on strength of feeling. Most of them are practised in section B of the unit.

Answers: 2   4   5   1 (or 3)   3 (or 1)

A3 Friday the thirteenth

This is a *matching exercise*. Follow the same general procedure as for unit 1, A2 'Best wishes' (see notes, p. 27).

This exercise presents typical formulae for apologising in letters. The expressions especially show differences in formality, which correspond to different relationships (e.g. lover, close friend, acquaintance, official).

Answers
a) Embassy reception   b) Susie   c) Archie   d) Bank manager   e) Mr and Mrs Sweeney   f) Council meeting

Unit 9 Part two

SECTION B: PRACTICE

> Basic structures
> past perfect tense (B1)
> should + have done (B1)
> tag questions (B2)
> indirect questions (B2)

B1 One thing after another

Language function: Regretting things you have done.

Structural difficulties: Use of *I wish* + past perfect tense, for regretting *past* actions (cf. unit 1).

Procedure: Follow the same general procedure as for unit 1, B1 'Wishful thinking' (see notes, p. 28).

Stage 1 Example answers
  'I wish/If only I hadn't got so drunk.'
  'I should never have drunk so much.'
  'I should have kept to beer.'
  'Why on earth did I lose my temper?'
  'Whatever made me shout at my boss?'
  'What a fool I was to drive so fast.'
  'I can't think why I was so rude to Sally.'

Stage 2 The three pictures are intentionally ambiguous. Discuss possible interpretations before doing the exercise (e.g. picture 1: The man might be the owner of the house, a thief who's been caught, someone who's been kidnapped, etc.).

Note: This exercise can also be used to practise past conditional structures:
  e.g. 'If I'd set the alarm, I wouldn't have been late.'
  'If I hadn't been given the sack, I wouldn't have driven so dangerously.'
  'If I hadn't had a row with Sally, none of this would have happened.'

B2 What a let down

Language functions: Expressing disappointment; agreeing.

Structural difficulties
1 Structure and usage of *(not) worth . . . -ing*. Notice that this is often followed by a 'hanging preposition' (without 'it') e.g. 'It wasn't worth going to.'
2 The exercise involves quite complicated *as . . . as . . .* structures, which may need special presentation and practice.
e.g. 'It wasn't as good as I thought it would be.'
'It wasn't as exciting as the papers said it was.'

Procedure
Stage 1 Go through the expressions with the class, asking students to complete them.
Stage 2 Each of the expressions can be used either in the opening remark or in the reply. Before doing the pairwork practice, make sure the class knows what tags to use in each reply.
Stage 3 Students improvise similar two-line conversations for the other situations. Insist that they use different structures from the list each time, so that they practise the whole range of expressions.

B3 Manwick depression

Language functions: Expressing dissatisfaction with your own situation and disillusionment with the way things have turned out; expressing sympathy and giving advice.

Structural difficulties: None.

Procedure: This is a *skeleton conversation.* Follow the same general procedure as for unit 2, B3 'Have you heard?' (see notes, p. 39).

Stage 1 Possible answers
   Carol: 'What, it's the exams, is it?'
   'Don't worry. The exams will be over soon.'
   Martin: 'It's the work. I don't seem to be able to concentrate any more.'
   'It's the social life. Sometimes I get the feeling that it's all rather artificial.'
   'It's people's attitudes around here. I'm beginning to think I came to the wrong university.'
Stage 2 Prepare for the pairwork by discussing what each of the other three students' problems might be.
The 'skeleton' is only the opening of the conversation. Students should try to develop each one into a brief discussion.

Unit 9 Part two

Stage 3 As a round-up to the exercise, ask students to report briefly on what their problems were and what advice (if any) Carol gave.

SECTION C: FREE EXPRESSION

C1 Second thoughts

Language functions: Expressing disillusionment with the lifestyle you have chosen; regretting past actions; accusing and blaming.

This exercise gives further practice of the language introduced in B1 and B3.

This is a *group interview*. Follow the same general procedure as for unit 7, C1 'More Manwick developments' (see notes, p. 84).

C2 A bad move

Language function: Expressing disappointment and regret in writing.

This exercise gives further practice of the language introduced in B1 and B2.

This is a *guessing game*. Follow the same general procedure as for unit 1, C2 'Just the job' (see notes, p. 32).

No model is given in the Student's Book. Below is a model you can read out for the class to guess if you think it necessary:
'... I'm very disappointed with the new house. The walls are so thin you can hear everything that's happening next door, and, of course, all the houses are exactly the same. I wish I still had the old place – then I could take my home with me wherever I went. The worst thing is that I couldn't keep the old horse because the neighbours complained ...'
Answer: He's moved from the *gipsy caravan* to the *modern terraced house*.

Unit 10 Interest/Curiosity

Part one: Talking about the feeling

SECTION A: LISTENING AND DISCUSSION

A1 **Listening** and **A2** **Facts**

Procedure (For more detail on procedure see notes on unit 1, p. 19.)
Stage 1 Books closed. Play the dialogue once.
Stage 2 Elicit information, playing the tape again where necessary.
Stage 3 Books open. Students follow as tape is played again.
Stage 4 Facts questions are answered briefly to summarise the preceding discussion.

Answers
1 They're strangers.
2 They're in a train.
3 A tape-recorder and/or microphone.
4 He's researching into linguistics.
   A linguist or a student.
5 He's stopping and rewinding the tape.
6 That his own voice has been recorded, as part of the research.

A3 **Language**

Procedure (For more detail on procedure see notes on unit 1, p. 21.)
Stage 1 Students answer the questions individually or in pairs.
Stage 2 Go through the answers with the whole class.

Answers
1 a,b   c = interested in other people's business, e.g. 'He's a very inquisitive person.'
        You cannot be inquisitive *to* . . .
2 b
3 a,b,d c: you are *curious to know* or *curious about*.

102

Unit 10 Part one

     a,b,d: for meaning differences, see B1 'Shades of interest', below.
4 a For the difference between *interested in* and *interested by*, see B1 'Shades of interest', below.
5 b,d b and d = interested in a *bad* sense.
     b is less formal than d.
6 a,b,d a, b and d all mean that he *agrees* to play it, he *has no objections* to playing it.
     e = he *has* to play it.

SECTION B: PRACTICE

B1 Shades of interest

Procedure
Stage 1 Go through the example with the class. Point out that the three alternative structures given can be used with many other feelings verbs and adjectives (for a full list see appendix B, p. 133).
Note: Emily was interested in/by the stranger.
interested in = she finds him an interesting person
(e.g. 'He's very interested in nuclear physics.')
interested by = her interest is suddenly aroused
(e.g. 'I was interested by what you said just now about nuclear fission.')
Stage 2 Discuss the meanings of the other three adjectives:
fascinated = something catches and holds your attention.
intrigued = you don't fully understand something and want to find out more about it.
bored = not interested, fed up.
Stage 3 Students practise the alternative forms by manipulating the three 'Emily' sentences.
Stage 4 In groups or pairs, students talk about the six other people in the exercise. Make sure they use a variety of forms in their answers.
Answers
a) intrigued b) interested c) fascinated
d) intrigued e) bored f) fascinated/intrigued
Stage 5 Relating the language to the dialogue:
Harry: 'I was intrigued by the tape-recorder he was holding.'
    'I find the idea of recording people on trains fascinating.'

Unit 10 Part one

James: 'I am very interested in linguistics.'

B2 Story line

Procedure
Stage 1 Go through the example with the class.
Stage 2 In groups or pairs, students make similar reports for the other three pictures.
Stage 3 Go through the answers with the whole class. Ask students to tell similar stories about themselves.
Stage 4 Relating the language to the dialogue:
James: 'He must have been wondering why I was holding a microphone.'
'He was obviously curious to know what the tape-recorder was for.'

SECTION C: REPORTING

C1 *The list.* Get students to suggest ways in which either Harry or James might use the listed expressions to tell the story of what happened.

Suggested answers
1 Both: 'He/I had a tape-recorder on the seat beside him/me.'
2 Harry: 'I couldn't make out what he was doing.'
  James: 'He obviously couldn't make out what I was doing.'
3 Both: 'He/I couldn't take his/my eyes off the tape-recorder.'
4 Both: 'He/I played back the tape (to me/him).'
5 Both: 'Eventually I/he plucked up courage and asked him/me ... '
  (= overcame his/my nervousness)
6 Harry: 'Apparently he's a linguist.'
  (= he told me he's a linguist)

C2 *Reporting.* Students now write reports, either individually, in pairs or groups, or for homework. Approximately half the reports should be from Harry's point of view, and half from James's point of view.

Two possible reports
Harry: 'There was a man in my compartment doing something with a tape-recorder. There wasn't any sound coming out — I couldn't make out what he was up to at all. I didn't want to seem too inquisitive, but eventually I got

Unit 10 Part two

            so curious that I plucked up courage and asked him. Well, apparently he was a linguist, or something. He was making a study of what people say on trains. I was really fascinated by the idea — I didn't realise people did things like that. He agreed to play some back to me, and when he switched it on you'll never guess what I heard — my own voice, asking him what he was doing with his tape-recorder!'

James: 'I had the tape-recorder on the train the other day, hoping to record some conversation for my thesis. There was a man sitting opposite me who was obviously very curious to know what I was doing. He couldn't take his eyes off the tape-recorder. Eventually he plucked up courage and asked me about it. I told him, and he seemed really interested in the study. Then he wanted to hear some of the tape. So I played him back his own voice, which I'd been recording all the time. You should've seen his face!'

Part two: Expressing the feeling

SECTION A: RECOGNITION

A1 Tell me more

Follow the same general procedure as for unit 1, A1 'Who wants what?' (see notes, p. 25). The remarks are all replies.

Suggested answers
1. Someone is listening to a long story. Reply to 'I hope I'm not boring you.'
2. Someone being shown a typewriter, e.g. in a shop. Reply to e.g. 'And this little button pops up when you're getting near the bottom of the page.'
3. Someone is being told about a conversation that he's very interested in. Reply to e.g. 'And then I said . . . '
4. Someone listening to a story about e.g. a car breakdown. Reply to e.g. 'There wasn't much we could do, really.'
5. At a social gathering, e.g. a party. About something the other

Unit 10 Part two

person is wearing, or one of his/her possessions. Reply to e.g. 'Have you noticed the icon, by the way?'
6 The other person has just raised a subject which the speaker had forgotten about. Reply to e.g. 'Oh. I haven't told you about the interview, have I?'
7 The two people are talking about a mysterious stranger. A trusts him, but B distrusts him. Reply to e.g. 'They seem to be a perfectly respectable family to me.'
8 Miss Whippet has just told a policeman about an incident involving a car with the registration number KBK 125F. The policeman becomes more interested since he recognises the number. Reply to 'Let me see . . . Yes it was KBK 125F.'

Other feelings: 3 impatience   4 sympathy   7 suspicion
                    8 surprise

A2 It's not what you say...

This is a *matching exercise* concerned with differences in intonation (see also unit 8, A2 'In a manner of speaking').

This exercise introduces the use of *'positive' tag questions*, which are typically used in making initial contacts with other people, showing you are interested, and 'feeding' them to tell you more about themselves. The precise function of 'positive' tag questions depends on the way they are said; those demonstrated on the tape are:
1 registering a fact that is already known (a,e)
2 suddenly realising, making a deduction (b,c)
3 expressing doubt or suspicion (d)

Procedure: Follow the same general procedure as for 'In a manner of speaking' in unit 8 (see notes, p. 90).

Answers: 1 d   2 b   3 a   4 e   5 c

A3 Skeleton in the cupboard

This is a *multiple-choice conversation*. There is another exercise like this in unit 11 (p. 115). *Note:* The tape gives the answers: use only at the round-up stage.

The main purpose of the exercise is to give insight into differences in appropriacy; all three choices for A are grammatically correct, but only one of his remarks each time is entirely appropriate in the context. Two general features are especially important:

Unit 10 Part two

i) Because Frank is trying to get Arthur to talk about an embarrassing subject, he has to be cautious in what he says; but they are old friends, so he won't use highly formal language.
ii) These are not isolated remarks, but a developing conversation; so Frank's remarks must be appropriate as responses to what Arthur says.

Procedure

Stage 1 Explain the purpose of the exercise, and make sure that the class clearly understands the situation.

Stage 2 Divide the class into pairs or groups. As with other recognition exercises, students should not only choose the correct answer, but also discuss why the others are inappropriate.

Stage 3 Go through the answers with the class. The exercise contains key expressions for *showing interest without giving offence*. These should be presented at this point:
................., I suppose?
................., + positive tag
positive tag questions

Answers
1 a) Correct.
 b) Wrong. Friends would use this for something much more personal e.g. whether someone's marriage is going wrong.
 c) Wrong. This would only be said if Arthur had refused to tell him, and would not go with 'By the way'.
2 a) Wrong. This would mean that Frank is correcting Arthur.
 b) Wrong. This would mean 'I've suddenly remembered that ... '
 c) Correct. This is similar to (a) in A2 'It's not what you say', above.
3 a) Wrong. He would say this if they were both wondering about someone else, i.e. 'I wonder why he did that?'
 b) Correct.
 c) Wrong. It sounds like an order.
4 a) Wrong. This is like 3(a), above.
 b) Correct.
 c) This is appropriate, but Arthur's reply does not

Unit 10 Part two

fit. He would be more likely to say 'No, that wasn't it', or 'It wasn't that exactly'.

Stage 4 As a round-up/reinforcement stage, students can read or improvise the conversation in pairs, after listening to the tape.

SECTION B: PRACTICE

> Basic structures
> indirect questions (B1, B3)
> gerunds (B1)
> *must + have done* (B1)

B1 The Old Curiosity Shop

Language functions: Showing curiosity about something you see; speculating and making deductions.

Structural difficulties: None.
The expressions practised in this exercise are of three kinds:
1 expressing surprise ('Fancy . . . !' 'Imagine . . . !')
2 wondering ('I wonder . . . ', 'Do you think . . . ?')
3 speculating and deducing ('I bet', 'I expect', 'Presumably', 'They must've')

Procedure
Stage 1 Go through the expressions, and ask students to use them for each of the five topics in the list.
Example answers
'Fancy having to carry that all the way upstairs!'
'They must've used it as a hot-water bottle, or something.'
'I wonder what they used it for?'
'I bet the stopper didn't work very well.'
'I expect everybody used them a hundred years ago.'
'Do you think it's worth much?'
'Presumably they took it out before they got into bed.'
Stage 2 Divide the class into pairs or groups. They speculate in a similar way about the objects in the pictures, using the five topics in the list as a guide.
Stage 3 To round up the exercise, ask each group what they

Unit 10 Part two

thought the object was, and what speculations they made about it.
Note: It is important that the main object of the exercise is *not* just to identify the object, but to speculate further about it.
The three objects are:
1 coffee maker   2 stays   3 clothes press

B2 Gossip column

Language function: Reacting with interest to something someone tells you.

Structural difficulties: None.

Procedure
Stage 1 Discuss what the story is about. Students should be able to establish that it is a piece of gossip or scandal, and that it is about a family they know. An imaginative class may be able to think up a detailed story that would fit the replies.
Stage 2 An important aspect of this exercise is the ability to *react appropriately* and *interrupt* to show you are interested. A good way to practise this before the pairwork stage is for the teacher to tell a story, pausing every now and then so that the students can react.
Stage 3 Divide the class into pairs. Working together, each pair makes up a piece of gossip, making brief notes if necessary.
Stage 4 Students form new pairs. One student in each pair tells his story, and the other shows his interest. Then they change roles.

B3 Between strangers

Language function: Expressing curiosity in formal situations, without giving offence.

Structural difficulties: Point out to the class that items a,b,d,f and g are followed by *indirect question* structures, even though they end with question marks. The other items are, of course, direct questions.

The expressions are of two types:
i) Those used for asking about things which are not personal:

Excuse me. Could you tell me ... ?
Excuse me. Do you happen to know ... ?
Excuse me. I wonder if you could tell me ... ?
Excuse me. I don't suppose you know ... do you?
Excuse me. Do you think you could tell me?
(Also used for practice situations c, d and e)
ii) Those used for asking about personal things, which might suggest you are being inquisitive:
Excuse me. I don't want to seem inquisitive, but ... ?
Excuse me. I hope you don't mind me asking, but ... ?
Excuse me. I hope you don't think I'm being inquisitive, but ... ?
(Also used for practice situations a, b and f)
The pairwork should take the form of a freely improvised conversation, beginning with remarks from the list.

SECTION C: FREE EXPRESSION

C1 Touchy subject

Language functions: Finding out about something without seeming too obviously inquisitive; being evasive.

This exercise gives further practice of language introduced in A3.

This is a *half-and-half improvisation.* Follow the same general procedure as for unit 2, C1 'Old and new' (see notes, p. 40).

C2 What on Earth?

Language functions. Showing curiosity about something you see; speculating.

This exercise gives further practice of language introduced in B1.

This is a *guessing game.* Follow the same general procedure as for unit 1, C2 'Just the job' (see notes, p. 32).
Answer to the example: They're examining a saucepan.

Unit 11 Uncertainty

Part one: Talking about the feeling

SECTION A: LISTENING AND DISCUSSION

A1 Listening and **A2 Facts**

Procedure (For more detail on procedure see notes on unit 1, p. 19.)
Stage 1 Books closed. Play the dialogue once.
Stage 2 Elicit information, playing the tape again where necessary.
Stage 3 Books open. Students follow as tape is played again.
Stage 4 Facts questions are answered briefly to summarise the preceding discussion.

Answers
1 Karl: a student of English.
   Ernest: a teacher of English.
2 In a classroom.
3 A grammar exercise, probably of the 'Put in the article where necessary' type.
4 A question in the exercise. Probably ' ___ people in England drink tea'.
5 He tries to explain when to use 'the' and when not to.
6 Because he hasn't understood anything, and is not sure what to say.

A3 Language

Procedure (For more detail on procedure see notes on unit 1, p. 21.)
Stage 1 Students answer the questions individually or in pairs.
Stage 2 Go through the answers with the whole class.

Answers
1 a,b,c   d is too strong. See B1 'In the dark', below.
2 b,d   a is old-fashioned. Nowadays it usually means 'to calculate'.

Unit 11 Part one

	c would be followed by 'about' (+ noun or indirect question); it would also imply that Karl had discussed it with someone else.
3 a,c	You explain *something* (*to* somebody).
4 a,c	b and d would mean that he had given a full and clear explanation.
5 b,d	*realise* and *know* are not used with *can't*: Karl realises/ knows *that* Ernest is giving an explanation, but he doesn't *understand* that explanation.
6 b,c	*puzzled* is too weak, and is not an absolute adjective.
7 c,d	Ernest is giving the explanation, and he gets confused/ mixed up. It is Karl who is at first *puzzled*, and later, *baffled*.

SECTION B: PRACTICE

B1 In the dark

Procedure

Stage 1 Go through the examples with the class. Make sure they understand the differences between the three adjectives.
If you're *baffled*, you're more than puzzled. You haven't got the slightest idea what the answer is.
If you're *confused*, your thoughts are all mixed up. You can't think clearly.

Stage 2 In pairs or groups, students talk about the other people in the exercise.

Stage 3 Go through the answers with the whole class.
Answers
1 baffled   2 puzzled   3 confused   4 puzzled
5 confused   6 baffled   7 baffled (and confused)

Stage 4 Relating the language to the dialogue:
Both: 'I/Karl was puzzled by number 5.'
'I/He tried to explain, but I/he got confused.'
'By the end, I/Karl was utterly baffled.'

B2 Shades of meaning

Procedure

Stage 1 Go through the examples with the class.

Stage 2 In pairs or groups, students talk about the five people in the exercise.

Unit 11 Part one

Stage 3   Go through the answers with the whole class.
          Answers
          1 Jock couldn't work out how to solve the problem.
          2 Elspeth couldn't make out who the man was.
          3 Harold couldn't tell whether he was eating margarine or butter.
            Harold couldn't tell the difference between margarine and butter.
          4 Margery couldn't work out/make out why the man was standing there.
          5 Richard couldn't tell from the photograph which town it was.
Stage 4   Relating the language to the dialogue:
          Both: 'I/Karl couldn't work out whether I/he should put "the" or not.'
                'I/Karl couldn't make out what he/I was trying to say.'

SECTION C: REPORTING

C1 *The list.* Get students to suggest ways in which Karl or Ernest might use the listed expressions to tell the story of what happened.

Suggested answers
1 Karl: 'We were doing an exercise on articles.'
           'I wasn't sure whether to put the article in or not.'
  Ernest: 'I gave them an exercise on articles.'
2 Ernest: 'I tried to clarify the point for him.'
3 Karl: 'He went into a long-winded explanation.'
  Ernest: 'I'm afraid I must have been a bit long-winded.'
           (= unnecessarily long and complicated)
4 Karl: 'He went on and on.'
           (= he kept talking)
           'He kept going on about cows.'
5 Karl: 'I didn't really get the point of what he was saying.'
  Ernest: 'It seemed as if he still hadn't got the point.'
6 Karl: 'I couldn't make head or tail of what he was saying.'
           (= couldn't understand it at all)

C2 *Reporting.* Students now write reports, either individually, in pairs or groups, or for homework. Approximately half the reports should be from Karl's point of view and half from Ernest's point of view.

Two possible reports

Karl: 'We were doing an exercise on articles this morning, when I got to number 5, which said "___ people in England drink tea". I wasn't very sure about it — I couldn't make up my mind whether it should be "people" or "the people". So I asked Mr Potts about it. Instead of just telling me the answer, he began a terribly long-winded, complicated explanation about articles in general. I couldn't make head or tail of it — it was something about people in class and cows in a field, I think. And then, when I suggested "the people", he said no and started going on about people in a class again. And finally he said that it was "the people" after all . . . I was puzzled at the beginning, but by the end I was completely baffled — and to tell you the truth, I think he was getting a bit confused himself. So I thought I'd ask you . . . '

Ernest: 'I gave the class an exercise on articles this morning. I noticed young Karl looking a bit puzzled, so I went over and offered to help. I wish I hadn't! He wasn't sure whether number 5 should be "People in England drink tea" or "The people in England drink tea". Karl's an intelligent boy, so I thought I'd try to explain the underlying principles of the thing rather than just tell him the answer. It was all right at first — I gave him a couple of examples — but then I realised that he hadn't really got the point I was trying to make. I tried to clarify things a bit more, but it was obvious that the poor boy was completely confused. And what's more, I was getting a bit mixed up myself. So I thought I'd just give him the answer and leave it at that. The trouble is, I've just realised that I gave him the *wrong* answer. You see, I thought . . . '

Unit 11 Part two

Part two: Expressing the feeling

SECTION A: RECOGNITION

A1 Muddled minds

Follow the same general procedure as for unit 1, A1 'Who wants what?' (see notes, p. 25).

Suggested answers
1 Teacher being visited by parent of one of the students. He can't remember the parent's name or much about the student.
2 Palaeontologist or zoologist, looking at a fossil, and not being sure what it is.
3 Householder to man at the door, who claims to be from the Electricity Board and wants to come in and read the meters.
4 Embarrassed employer, about to sack an employee, but not sure how to break the news to him.
5 Someone trying to solve a crossword clue, which has two equally good answers (both anagrams of 'heads').
6 Someone trying to follow a recipe which doesn't have very clear instructions.
7 Someone who thought he was talking to the new secretary, and suddenly begins to wonder whether he is.

A2 Mental block

Note: The tape gives the answers: use only at the round-up stage.

This is a *multiple-choice conversation*. Follow the same general procedure as for unit 10, A3 'Skeleton in the cupboard' (see notes, p. 106).

Answers
1 a) Wrong. Doesn't fit in with A's next remark.
   b) Wrong. 'Think' should be made negative, as in answer (c).
   c) Correct.
2 a) Wrong. This is either a response to a query, or a way of correcting someone.
   b) Correct.
   c) This would indicate that he has realised that he is wrong.
3 a) Wrong. A isn't confusing — what she says is confusing.
   b) Wrong. You cause confusion, you don't cause *someone* confusion. e.g. 'The news caused a lot of confusion in political circles.'

Unit 11 Part two

      c) Correct.
4 a) Correct.
   b) Much too definite, and rather awkward.
   c) Wrong. 'Of course' would mean either 'as you know' or 'I've just remembered', as in 'One of them went abroad. But of course that was Michael, Sam's brother.'

A3 Ambivalent answers

This exercise introduces language used in hesitating and changing one's mind. The expressions are on a scale from 'fairly certain' to 'completely uncertain'.

Follow the same procedure as for *matching exercises* (see notes for 'Best wishes' in unit 1, p. 27).

Answers
a) e.g. 'Who's this poem by?'
b) least uncertain: 1 3 4 2 :most uncertain

A useful extension to this exercise is for students to practise answering 'tricky' questions, using the expressions in the example. The teacher can fire questions at individual students, and they can then ask each other questions in pairs.

SECTION B: PRACTICE

Basic structures
looks like + noun (B1)
looks as if + clause (B1)
might/could + *be* (B1)
may/might + *have done* (B2)

B1 Unusual angles

Language functions: Trying to interpret something you see; disagreeing.

Structural difficulties: None.

Procedure
Stage 1 Look at the picture with the class, and ask students to guess what it is, using the expressions in the bubbles.

Unit 11 Part two

Answer: It's a pile of coins (10p pieces).

Stage 2 Before going on to the other three pictures, go through the expressions in the box, which are used for *disagreeing* and suggesting an *alternative opinion*.

Stage 3 In pairs, students look at the other three pictures and discuss what they might be. The importance of the exercise is, of course, in talking about the picture rather than finding the right answer. Since students will be uncertain what the pictures are, the key expressions should come naturally into what they say about them. The three pictures are:
1 milk-bottle top
2 milk splash
3 mascara brush

B2 Alibi

Language function: Being uncertain about the past; not being able to remember.

Structural difficulties: None.

Procedure

Stage 1 Read through the person's answers. Establish what the situation is, and what questions he is being asked. The questions could be:
'When did you get home from work?'
'Are you sure it was 5 o'clock?'
'And what did you do when you got home?'
'What programme did you watch?'
'Did you go out at all during the evening?'
'What time was that?'
'Do you remember what you were wearing?'

Stage 2 Ask students to pick out expressions indicating uncertainty. These are central to the exercise, and can be built up on the board:
Well, let's see ...
I'm not quite sure.
I really couldn't tell you.
As far as I remember ...
I suppose/think/don't think ...
I have a feeling ...
may/might/could, etc.

Stage 3 Divide the class into pairs. They 'interrogate' each other about their actions over the last twenty-four hours. It

Unit 11 Part two

is important that they ask each other *very detailed* questions. This stage can be set up as a role-play activity, with A as a policeman and B as a suspect.

B3   At a loss

Language functions: Being unable to decide what to do; making suggestions; rejecting suggestions.

Structural difficulties
1 Use of *try* + *-ing*
2 Amy's last remark, *'Unless perhaps . . .'* is likely to be followed by the *past tense*, to express a hypothetical idea, e.g. 'Unless perhaps I *moved* the piano into the bedroom.'

Procedure: This is a *skeleton conversation.* Follow the same general procedure as for unit 2, B3 'Have you heard?' (see notes, p. 39). As in other units, the 'skeleton' is only the beginning of the conversation. In the pairwork stage, encourage students to develop it into an extended discussion. Round the exercise up by asking students what solutions they found, if any. Here is a possible version of the conversation:

Amy: The thing is, I've no idea where I'm going to put them all.
Bob: Hmm. Have you thought of using the garden?
Amy: Hmm, I could do, I suppose — but I don't want to disturb the neighbours, really.
Bob: Oh, I see — yes, it might be a bit noisy. Well, you might try taking all the furniture out of your bedroom and using that as an extra room.
Amy: Oh, I couldn't do that — I don't want all those people smoking in my bedroom.
Bob: Oh, well, I don't know what to suggest, then.
Amy: Unless perhaps you took some of the chairs back to your place . . .

SECTION C: FREE EXPRESSION

C1   Images

Language function: Trying to interpret something you see.

This exercise gives further practice of the language introduced in B1.

Unit 11 Part two

Procedure: This should be done as a group discussion, and should be left completely free. After the discussion stage *either*
- a) ask each group what conclusions they came to
- *or* b) form new groups (each containing a representative from each original group). They can then discuss and compare the conclusions that the different groups came to.

The actual title of the picture is: 'The Therapist'.

C2 Labour saving devices

Language functions: Explaining a process; being uncertain how to explain a process.

Procedure

Stage 1 Divide the class into groups. Either give each group one machine to invent, or let them choose one of the five machines. Working together, they work out in detail what their machine would look like and how it would work. They may draw a rough diagram to help them.

Stage 2 Two students from each group move to the next group. They explain their machine, as far as possible *without* using diagrams. The listeners should ask as many awkward questions as possible!

Unit 12 Sympathy and lack of sympathy

Part one: Talking about the feeling

SECTION A: LISTENING AND DISCUSSION

A1 **Listening** and **A2** **Facts**

Procedure (For more detail on procedure see notes on unit 1, p. 19.)
Stage 1 Books closed. Play the dialogue once.
Stage 2 Elicit information, playing the tape again where necessary.
Stage 3 Books open. Students follow as tape is played again.
Stage 4 Facts questions are answered briefly to summarise the preceding discussion.

Answers
1 Friends, probably neighbours.
2 In Tony's house or flat.
3 His house has been broken into, and something of little value has been stolen or broken.
4 Because Tony isn't reacting to what he's saying.
5 His house has also been broken into, and his hi-fi, violin, a painting and some valuable old books have been stolen.
6 He's pointing at the space where his hi-fi used to be.
7 e.g. '... that they had broken in here too.'

A3 **Language**

Procedure (For more detail on procedure see notes on unit 1, p. 21.)
Stage 1 Students answer the questions individually or in pairs.
Stage 2 Go through the answers with the whole class.

Answers
1 b,e a and c: these imply that he's *working*.
       d: = you like someone/something, e.g. 'He's very taken with the new secretary.'
2 b,d a is also possible, but would better describe Tony's

120

Unit 12 Part one

attitude if he had said 'It's your own fault.' See B1 'Fellow feeling', below.
c = *unbiased, not taking sides.*

3 a   b = *like*, or *look after.*
c = *look after.*

4 b,c   a: the *valuables* have been stolen, not the house.
c: *burgled* = broken into and robbed at night.

5 a,d,e b,c: see unit 9, B1, 'Feeling low' (p. 95).

6 a,c   b = very frightened.

7 a,b   c: = present participle of the verb 'sympathise'. It is not used as an adjective.

SECTION B: PRACTICE

B1 Fellow feeling

Procedure

Stage 1 Go through the examples with the class, and ask them to match the people and the comments a–f.
Answers: Donald: d,e   David: a,c,f   Danny: b,f
(*Note:* f appears twice because 'he wasn't sympathetic' can mean *either* he was unsympathetic (i.e. he said it was my fault) *or* just that he didn't show any feeling of sympathy (i.e. he wasn't interested).)

Stage 2 In groups or pairs, students use the expressions to talk about the reactions of Frank's friends to his bad news. To add variety, students could continue their answers with *about* or *that*.
e.g. 'Hugh was most unsympathetic when I told him about the fight/that I'd broken my arm.'
Answers
a) most unsympathetic, not in the least sympathetic
b) not very sympathetic
c) most sympathetic, full of sympathy
d) most sympathetic, full of sympathy
e) not very sympathetic, completely indifferent, not in the least sympathetic
f) most unsympathetic, not in the least sympathetic
g) not very sympathetic

Stage 3 Relating the language to the dialogue:
Mark: 'When I told Tony about the burglary, he was completely indifferent.'

Unit 12 Part one

Tony: 'When Mark realised what had happened to me, he was full of sympathy.'

B2 **Story line**

Procedure
Stage 1 Go through the examples with the class.
Stage 2 In groups or pairs, students make similar reports, two for each of the situations given.
Stage 3 Go through the answers with the whole class.
Stage 4 Relating the language to the dialogue:
Tony: 'I was feeling really depressed after the burglary. Mark came in and started telling me all about his broken window, and obviously had no idea that I'd lost almost everything I possessed. Anyway, I was so preoccupied with my own problems that I'm afraid I couldn't really take in what he was saying.'
Mark: 'I started telling Tony about the burglary, but he didn't seem to care at all. In fact, he just sat there and ignored what I was saying about my carpet. Then I noticed that his hi-fi wasn't there any more, and it suddenly dawned on me that he must have been robbed too.'

SECTION C: REPORTING

C1 *The list.* Get students to suggest ways in which either Mark or Tony might use the listed expressions to tell the story of what happened.

Suggested answers
1 Both: 'Someone broke into my house last night.'
   Mark: 'I suddenly realised that his house had been broken into as well.'
2 Mark: 'He didn't show much/any interest in what I was saying.'
3 Mark: 'Whenever I spoke to him, he just mumbled in reply.'
4 Mark: 'It didn't occur to me that his place could have been burgled too.'
5 Tony: 'When he realised what had happened, he was very apologetic.'
6 Tony: 'Poor Mark. He was so embarrassed when he saw how much I'd lost.'

Unit 12 Part one

Mark: 'Poor Tony. I was so embarrassed when I saw how little I'd lost compared to him.'

C2 *Reporting.* Students now write reports, either individually, in pairs or groups, or for homework. Approximately half the reports should be from Mark's point of view, and half from Tony's point of view.

Two possible reports

Mark: '... As soon as the police left, I went over the road to Tony's to tell him about it. He didn't seem his usual self somehow, and wasn't the least bit sympathetic when I told him about the burglary — he just sat there looking miserable. I was so taken up with my story that it was some time before I realised that anything was wrong. Then, when I asked him what the matter was, he just pointed to the space where his hi-fi should have been. He'd been robbed too! And they'd taken all sorts of valuables — pictures, books, everything. I felt really embarrassed, after going on so much about my own problems — after all, it was only a broken window. So I sat and tried to cheer him up for a bit ...'

Tony: '... Mark's house was burgled too, of course — in fact he came round this morning and started going on and on about what they'd stolen from him — practically nothing, as far as I could tell, though I was feeling far too depressed about my own losses to start sympathising with him. Anyway, he was so taken up with his own little problems that he didn't even notice that nearly everything I owned had been stolen. It took him some time before he realised that there was anything the matter with me at all. When I did tell him what had happened, though, he was most sympathetic. He forgot all about his broken window and his carpet, and really did his best to cheer me up ...'

Unit 12 Part two

Part two: Expressing the feeling

SECTION A: RECOGNITION

A1 Cause for concern

Follow the same general procedure as for unit 1, A1 'Who wants what?' (see notes, p. 25).

Suggested answers
1 Not sympathetic. Something has been lost, destroyed, stolen, etc. The speaker is pointing out that it isn't so bad since the loss is covered by insurance.
2 Sympathetic. One player of an outdoor game (e.g. tennis, archery, golf) to another, who has just made a bad shot on a windy day.
3 Unsympathetic. To someone who entered a competition and lost.
4 Sympathetic. Written or formal way of expressing sympathy to someone whose close relative has just died.
5 Sympathetic. The speaker thinks that someone who has been sent to prison has been given too heavy a sentence.
6 Sympathetic. The newspapers have got hold of a story of a man involved in some kind of scandal, and have made a big sensation out of it.
7 Superficially sympathetic. Someone looking at or talking about baby animals which are used for food, e.g. lambs, calves, etc.
8 Sympathetic. Parent comforting small child who has lost a toy pig.

A2 A friend in need

This is a *matching exercise*. Follow the same general procedure as for unit 1, A2 'Best wishes' (see notes, p. 27).

This exercise presents basic formulae for reassuring people. The language varies according to what the *other person* is feeling and what he has just said.

Answers
1 Disappointed. Reply to e.g. 'What a pity. I wanted to stay in that hotel.'

Unit 12 Part two

2 Worried. Reply to e.g. 'I'm not looking forward to meeting her parents.'
3 Annoyed. Reply to e.g. 'Look at my carpet! He's burned a hole right through it!'
4 Depressed. Reply to e.g. 'I've a good mind to give up my job. It's getting so boring.'
5 Guilty. Reply to e.g. 'I should have been more careful. I could have prevented it then.'
6 Impatient. Reply to e.g. 'Where's that waiter? We've been here 20 minutes now.'

A3   Heart of stone

This is a *matching exercise*. Follow the same general procedure as for unit 1, A2 'Best wishes' (see notes, p. 27).

This exercise presents typical formulae for expressing indifference. Many of them would be considered impolite; students need to recognise them, but should be wary of using them.
The three types of response express:
a) indifference to what someone else is doing
b) indifference to someone who wants or asks for something
c) indifference to someone who feels sorry for himself.

Answers
a) 'It's no concern of mine.'
   'There's nothing I can do about it.'
   'It's none of my business.'
   'It's nothing to do with me.'
b) 'Search me.'
   'How should I know.'
   'Don't ask me.'
   'Haven't a clue.'
c) 'You've only yourself to blame.'
   'Serves you right.'
   'I'm not surprised.'
   'It's your own fault.'

SECTION B: PRACTICE

Basic structures
gerunds (B1, B3)
sequence of tenses (B1)

Unit 12 Part two

B1   For and against

Language function: Expressing sympathy and lack of sympathy for someone who has a problem.

Structural difficulties: Emphatic use of *will* (= must, insist on) in:
'Well, if you *will* buy houses that no one else wants!'
Notice that the expression is complete in itself; it could but doesn't have to be followed by e.g. '. . . you've only yourself to blame.'

Note: The situation is the same in each column, but the interaction is different:
Left column: Alfred blames himself, and his friend is sympathetic.
Right column: Alfred feels sorry for himself, and his friend is unsympathetic.

Procedure
Stage 1   Ask students to suggest as many reasons as possible why Alfred can't sell his house.
Possible reasons
Something's wrong with it (woodworm/rot/subsidence).
They've built a main road through his garden.
There's a slump in the market.
The house is too big and expensive to run.

Stage 2   Go through the replies and ask students to complete them.
Possible answers
a) 'How were you to know/You weren't to know there'd be a slump in the market.'
'It's hardly your fault/You can't help it if they closed the railway down.'
b) 'What do you expect if you ask so much for it?'
'I warned you about buying houses in this area.'
'Well, if you will buy houses without having a survey done first.'
'Well, you didn't have to buy such a big house, did you?'
'That's what happens when you buy a sixteenth-century mansion.'

Stage 3   Divide the class into pairs. They improvise two-line conversations based on the situations given, changing roles each time.

Unit 12 Part two

B2 Hard luck story

Language function: Showing you feel sorry for someone who has problems.

Structural difficulties: None.

Procedure

Stage 1   Establish what the situation is, and what the other person might be saying.
e.g. 'I've broken my leg . . .
. . . Well, I was coming down the stairs and I slipped and fell to the bottom . . .
. . . Well, it does hurt rather a lot, actually . . .
. . . That's just the trouble — she's in bed with tonsilitis . . .
. . . Yes, she's got a temperature of 102 — she can't even study . . .
. . . No, she has to stay in bed for at least a week, so I'm afraid she'll miss the exam . . .
. . . Oh no, they won't do that . . . '

Stage 2   Go through the key 'sympathy' expressions in the example, many of which are formulae:
e.g. I *am* sorry to hear that.
That *is* a shame.
That *is* bad luck.
It *would* have to happen now, wouldn't it?

Stage 3   Divide the class into pairs. They quickly act out the conversation in the example. Then, working together, they make up a 'hard luck story' of their own; this should be a combination of several problems, as in the example.

Stage 4   Students form new pairs. Each student tells his story to his new partner. The listener should sympathise as much as possible.

Stage 5   Further new pairs can be formed, and the process repeated.

B3 Other people's problems

Language functions: Expressing sympathy/lack of sympathy for someone else; disagreeing.

Structural difficulties: All the expressions in Stella's second example could be followed by infinitives, but are best followed by gerunds, as they refer to *repeated activities*.

Unit 12 Part two

Procedure: This is a *skeleton conversation*. Follow the same general procedure as for unit 2, B3 'Have you heard?' (see notes, p. 39).

Here is a possible version of the conversation:
Stella: Poor old Tom. Apparently he's been put on night shifts. He must be terribly fed up about it.
Donald: Oh, I don't know — he's not so badly off. After all, he'll be getting double pay.
Stella: Oh, come on. It can't be much fun getting home from work at six in the morning . . .

SECTION C: FREE EXPRESSION

C1 Schools of thought

Language functions: Expressing sympathy/lack of sympathy with other people; feeling people are right/wrong to behave as they did; criticising, disagreeing, arguing.

This is a *group interview*. Follow the same general procedure as for unit 7, C1 'More Manwick developments' (see notes, p. 84).

C2 Problem page

Language functions: Expressing anxiety and guilt; explaining a problem; seeking advice; expressing sympathy; giving advice.

Procedure
Stage 1 Ask students to suggest what Tongue-tied's problem might be, and how his letter might have sounded. A possible version:
'Dear Millie, My problem is that I find it difficult to express my feelings. I'm all right with strangers, but when I'm with someone I know well, I just dry up. I have a wonderful fiancée, whom I love very much, but whenever I want to tell her how I feel about her, the words just won't come out properly. What shall I do? Yours, Tongue-tied.'
Stage 2 Divide the class into groups. Working together, each group writes a short problem letter.
Stage 3 Pass each letter to the next group, who read it and write a sympathetic reply.
Stage 4 As a round-up to the exercise, one person from each group reads out the letter they received, and their reply to it.

Appendix A: The scope of each unit

This list shows the major functional areas covered by part two of each unit. Points of overlap between units are indicated by cross-references. Numbers in brackets refer to individual exercises.

Unit 1: Desire/Longing

1 Expressing desire to do something; wanting to have something (B2, C1)
2 Wishing for changes; longing for something to happen (B1) (see also unit 5, 'Irritation/Impatience')
3 Expressing dissatisfaction with your own situation (see also unit 9, 'Disappointment/Regret'); envying other people (see also unit 4, 'Admiration') (B3)
4 Imagining doing something you would like to do; fantasising (see also unit 2, 'Excitement/Anticipation') (B3, C2)
5 Hoping all goes well for someone else (A2)

Unit 2: Excitement/Anticipation

1 Looking forward to doing things (see also unit 1, 'Desire/Longing') (A2, B1)
2 Expressing excitement because something good is going to happen which will affect you (B3, C1)
3 Expressing excitement about what someone else is going to do (B2)
4 Being excited because you have just had an exciting idea (see also unit 6, 'Delight/Relief') (C2)
5 Being engaged in an exciting activity (A1)

Unit 3: Worry/Apprehension

1 Worrying about possible consequences of something that has happened to you (A2, B1)
2 Expressing anxiety about someone else (B2)
3 Expressing anxiety about your general situation (C1, C2)
4 Expressing apprehension about your own future; not looking forward to doing something; feeling nervous (B3)

Appendix A

5 Reassuring someone who is worried (see also unit 12 'Sympathy and lack of sympathy') (A2, B2, C1)

Unit 4: Admiration

1 Admiring things you see (see also unit 6, 'Delight/Relief') (B1, C2)
2 Complimenting people on their appearance (B2)
3 Admiring people for their achievements, congratulating (B2, C1, C2)
4 Expressing approval of other people's actions (B3)
5 Envying other people, their possessions, achievements, etc. (see also unit 6, 'Desire/Longing') (B2)

Unit 5: Irritation/Impatience

1 Expressing irritation with someone who persists in doing/not doing something (B1, C2)
2 Showing annoyance with someone who tries to make you do/stop you doing something (see also unit 7, 'Indignation/Annoyance') (B3)
3 Showing impatience because you are being obstructed, or things are not happening fast enough (see also unit 1, 'Desire/Longing') (A2, B2, C1)

Unit 6: Delight/Relief

1 Expressing delight because something good has happened to you (see also unit 2, 'Excitement/Anticipation'); expressing relief because you have finished/achieved something (B1)
2 Being glad you did/did not do something; expressing relief because of a 'narrow escape' (B1, B2)
3 Expressing delight with something you have or have been given; expressing gratitude and appreciation (see also unit 4, 'Admiration') (B3)
4 Expressing satisfaction with your own situation; being engaged in an enjoyable activity (C1, C2)
5 Expressing delight on meeting and leave-taking (A2)

Unit 7: Indignation/Annoyance

1 Accusing, blaming and criticising people when things have gone wrong (see also unit 12, 'Sympathy and lack of sympathy') (B1, C1)

Appendix A

2 Expressing indignation about other people's actions, and events beyond your control; expressing shock (see also unit 8, 'Surprise') (B2, C2)
3 Showing you are annoyed/offended because someone has let you down (see also unit 9, 'Disappointment/Regret') (B3)
4 Expressing indignation because someone does something he has no right to do, deliberately obstructs you, etc. (see also unit 5, 'Irritation/Impatience') (A2, C1)

Unit 8: Surprise

1 Expressing surprise when something you expected doesn't happen, or when something you didn't expect does happen (B1)
2 Reacting with surprise to something someone tells you (see also unit 10, 'Curiosity/Interest') (B2, C2)
3 Being surprised/puzzled by news you hear of someone else (see also unit 11, 'Uncertainty') (B3, C1)
4 Being shocked (see also unit 7, 'Indignation') (B2, B3)

Unit 9: Disappointment/Regret

1 Expressing disappointment with an experience (see also unit 7, 'Indignation') (B2)
2 Regretting things you have done or failed to do (A2, B1, C1, C2)
3 Expressing dissatisfaction with your own situation; expressing disillusionment with the way things have turned out (see also unit 1, 'Desire/Longing') (B3, C1)
4 Apologising for things you have/haven't done (A3)

Unit 10: Interest/Curiosity

1 Expressing curiosity about something you see; making enquiries (A2, B3)
2 Reacting with interest to something someone else tells you (see also unit 8, 'Surprise') (B2)
3 Expressing curiosity about something you see; speculating (see also unit 11, 'Uncertainty') (B1, C2)
4 Finding out about something without seeming too inquisitive: veiled curiosity (A3, C1)

Appendix A

Unit 11: Uncertainty

1 Being puzzled, baffled; being unable to interpret, assess, identify something (see also unit 8, 'Surprise' and unit 10, 'Curiosity/Interest') (B1, C1)
2 Being uncertain about the past; being unable to remember (B2)
3 Being unclear about facts, unable to explain something (A3, C2)
4 Being unable to decide what to do (B3)
5 Being confused; not following an explanation (A2)

Unit 12: Sympathy and lack of sympathy

1 Expressing sympathy and lack of sympathy for someone who has a problem (B1, B2, C2)
2 Expressing sympathy and lack of sympathy for other people's problems (A3, B3, C1)
3 Feeling people are right/wrong to behave as they did (see also unit 4, 'Admiration' and unit 7, 'Indignation/Annoyance') (C1)
4 Reassuring someone (A2, C2) (see also unit 3, 'Worry/Apprehension')

Appendix B: Adjectives and verbs used to describe feelings

This table shows:
1 what prepositions to use with adjectives that describe feelings.
2 equivalent verbs and adjectives that describe what *causes* the feeling.

Example

| I | felt / was | annoyed | about it. / with him. | He / It | annoyed me. | I found | him / it | annoying. |

---

*amazed by/to (hear) (8)	to amaze	amazing
angry about something/with someone (7)	(to anger)	—
annoyed about something/with someone (5, 7)	to annoy	annoying
anxious about (3)	—	—
anxious to (do) (1)	—	—
*astonished by/to (hear) (8)	to astonish	astonishing
*baffled by (11)	to baffle	baffling
bored by/with (10)	to bore	boring
concerned about (3)	—	—
(*)confused by (11)	to confuse	confusing
*delighted with/to (hear) (6)	to delight	delightful
*desperate to (do) (1)	—	—
disappointed with/by (9)	to disappoint	disappointing
(*)disillusioned with (9)	(to disillusion)	—
dissatisfied with (9)	to dissatisfy	unsatisfactory
eager to (do) (1)	—	—
excited about/by (2)	to excite	exciting
(*)fascinated by (10)	to fascinate	fascinating
frightened by (3)	to frighten	frightening
frustrated by/with (9)	to frustrate	frustrating
furious about something/with someone (7)	to infuriate	infuriating
glad about/to (hear) (6)	—	—
hurt by (7)	to hurt	(hurtful)
impatient with (5)	—	—
impressed by (4)	to impress	impressive
*indifferent to (12)	—	—
indignant about something/with someone (7)	—	—
interested by/in (10)	to interest	interesting
intrigued by (10)	to intrigue	intriguing
irritated by something/with someone (5)	to irritate	irritating
keen to (do) (1)	—	—
moved by (4)	to move	moving
nervous about (3)	—	—
offended by (7)	to offend	offensive
*overwhelmed by (4)	to overwhelm	overwhelming
pleased with/to (hear) (6)	(to please)	(pleasing)
puzzled by (11)	to puzzle	puzzling
relieved to (hear) (6)	—	—
(*)shocked by/to (hear) (8)	to shock	shocking
struck by (4)	(to strike)	striking

Appendix B

surprised by/to (hear) (8)	to surprise	surprising
sympathetic towards someone (12)	—	—
*terrified by (3)	to terrify	terrifying
*thrilled by/with (2)	to thrill	thrilling
unsympathetic towards someone (12)	—	—
worried about (3)	to worry	worrying

Adjectives marked * are 'absolutes', i.e. they describe a strong feeling and cannot be used with 'very', 'slightly', etc.

e.g. I was $\begin{vmatrix} slightly \\ very \end{vmatrix}$ annoyed with him.

I was *absolutely* furious with him.

Adjectives marked (*) can be used either as 'absolutes' or as normal adjectives.
Numbers in brackets refer to units in this book.

Appendix C: The cassette

Below is a complete list of items recorded on the accompanying cassette.

Unit 1: Part 1 A1: Dialogue
         Part 2 A1: Who wants what?

Unit 2: Part 1 A1: Dialogue
         Part 2 A1: Breathless moments

Unit 3: Part 1 A1: Dialogue
         Part 2 A1: A bundle of nerves
                A2: Lost in the post

Unit 4: Part 1 A1: Dialogue
         Part 2 A1: Good for you

Unit 5: Part 1 A1: Dialogue
         Part 2 A1: Sweet or sour?

Unit 6: Part 1 A1: Dialogue
         Part 2 A1: Feeling fine
                A2: Hello ... goodbye

Unit 7: Part 1 A1: Dialogue
         Part 2 A1: All steamed up
                A2: Going to extremes

Unit 8: Part 1 A1: Dialogue
         Part 2 A1: Surprise surprise
                A2: In a manner of speaking

Unit 9: Part 1 A1: Dialogue
         Part 2 A1: What's wrong?
                A2: Life at the top

Unit 10: Part 1 A1: Dialogue
         Part 2 A1: Tell me more
                A2: It's not what you say ...
                A3: Skeleton in the cupboard

Unit 11: Part 1 A1: Dialogue
         Part 2 A1: Muddled minds

Appendix C

                    A2: Mental block
                    A3: Ambivalent answers
Unit 12: Part 1 A1: Dialogue
        Part 2 A1: Cause for concern
               A2: A friend in need
               A3: Heart of stone